CAUGHT IN TIME

For Joan

This book has received financial support from the
Cultural Traditions Programme of the Community
Relations Council which aims to encourage
acceptance and understanding of cultural diversity.

The Friar's Bush Press,
24 College Park Avenue,
Belfast 7

First published 1986
Reprinted 1991

 Subsidised by the Arts Council of Northern Ireland

Book design — Spring Graphics, Saintfield
Typesetting — Compuset, Belfast
Halftone reproduction — Reprographics, Belfast
Printing — W. & G. Baird, Antrim

Caught in Time

W. A. MAGUIRE

THE PHOTOGRAPHS OF

Alex Hogg

OF BELFAST 1870 - 1939

Friar's Bush Press

ACKNOWLEDGEMENTS

THANKS ARE DUE first to the Trustees of the Ulster Museum for permission to publish the photographs from the A. R. Hogg Collection; then to the Museum's photographic staff — and especially Ron Holmes, who did most of the final work — for the excellence of the prints they produced from the original negatives and lantern slides.

For information about Hogg himself and the Hogg family I am grateful to Mr J. C. Hogg (who also kindly lent photographs for copying) and to Miss Agnes Matheson. Miss Muriel Hicks was very helpful in answering questions about her family's acquisition of Hogg's studio. A large number of people contributed usefully to the commentary, either by supplying answers to queries or by pointing me to useful sources. Among the many, I should mention particularly Dr A. Ewen and Dr J. McA. Taggart; Michael McCaughan and John Moore of the Ulster Folk & Transport Museum; Sheela Speers and Brian Kennedy; and the staffs of the Public Record Office of Northern Ireland, the Linen Hall Library and the Belfast Central Library (Irish and Local Studies section).

It seems scarcely decent to thank one's publisher, but Brian Walker of Friar's Bush Press is so knowledgeable about old photographs and their presentation that I am bound (in hard covers indeed) to record his help and also that of Margaret McNulty.

Most of all, however, I have to thank my colleagues in the Ulster Museum's department of Local History — Robert Heslip, Alfred Montgomery, Noel Nesbitt and Tom Wylie. They too have been living with Hogg for a long time. So has Pauline Cook, who typed and retyped the manuscript with her usual skill and good humour.

CONTENTS

Photographic Specialist
LANTERNIST & CINEMATOGRAPHER

Alex. R. Hogg

13 TRINITY STREET
Clifton Street
BELFAST

Telephone
2204

INTRODUCTION

SINCE 1939, when he died in his seventieth year, A. R. Hogg has been almost completely forgotten. Many of the details of his personal history are and will remain obscure, for he had no children and few close relatives, and there are no surviving family papers. A number of people recall him as he was in his latter years, but no one has been able to say much about his personal life to supplement the meagre evidence of newspaper obituaries. Indeed, it is somewhat ironic that we know so little, for it was Hogg who took the lead in assembling the R. J. Welch Collection (now in the Ulster Museum) as a memorial to his old friend and fellow photographer; and it was Hogg who played the leading part in promoting the activities of the Professional Photographers' Association in Ulster. Perhaps the date he died, only a few days before Hitler's invasion of Poland, helped to bury his memory along with his remains.

Yet Alex Hogg was a professional photographer in Belfast for almost forty years. At the time of his death he was the doyen of his profession, and only one other studio in the city had been in existence longer than his own. Not only that, he had a considerable—if mainly local—reputation. All this in itself might not be sufficient to justify his resurrection half a century later. Any professional photographer has to be competent if he is to last long in what has always been a fiercely competitive business; yet most, however competent, are quickly forgotten once they are gone, their stock of negatives scattered or destroyed. Fortunately we have a representative selection of Hogg's work, saved from destruction when the surviving contents of his studio were acquired by the Ulster Museum. More important, the range of the subject matter makes the collection particularly useful as an historical source, much more so than if he had earned his living taking portraits. Above all there is the superb quality of the photographs themselves. This volume presents a small selection of his best work.

The photographer photographed photographing: Hogg at work in the City Hall, Belfast in 1906, photographing the interior of the great dome of the new building from the floor of the entrance hall.

THE
PHOTOGRAPHER

ALEXANDER ROBERT HOGG was born on 1 March 1870 in the townland of Tullywest, which lies between Ballynahinch and Saintfield in County Down. His father David, second of the seven sons of Samuel and Elizabeth Hogg (both of whom died in 1895, he aged 91) was at that time a farmer. By the time his second son was born, in 1873, David Hogg had moved from Tullywest to the townland of Ballydollaghan in the parish of Drumbo, near Belfast. His occupation then was described as land steward; he was probably employed by the Batt family of Purdysburn, the leading local landowners. The only other child was a daughter, Mamie.

We know nothing about Alex Hogg's education and upbringing before he left home to serve his time as a druggist's assistant with his uncle James. James Hogg was the proprietor of a successful grocer's and druggist's business at 173 York Street, Belfast. As well as dispensing patent medicines such as Professor Brown's herbal remedies and 'The Acid Cure'—an incredibly useful 'external, safe, invaluable, certain cure for rheumatism, neuralgia, stomach, liver, kidney, chest fever and nervous complaints'—James Hogg was the inventor and wholesaler of his own 'Zulu' Insect Destroying Powder, guaranteed to kill 'beetles, crickets, bugs, fleas, moths, green flies, also insects in green or hot houses, vineries etc., without danger to human life or domestic animals'. Another uncle, Samuel, had a thriving grocery and provisions business

The earliest picture of Alex Hogg, aged about eighteen, when he was working as a druggist's apprentice with his uncle James in York Street. The photograph was taken by William Abernethy, whose High Street studio was still in business when Hogg died in 1939.

at 6-8 Shankill Road. A third worked in Belfast as a book-keeper. A fourth is said to have had a laundry business. Indeed, the family of old Samuel Hogg of Tullywest is typical of many a thrifty farming family in eastern Ulster in the nineteenth century in that most of the children emigrated to the city and joined the ranks of the commercial or white-collar middle class. In Hogg's own family the same thing happened in the next generation, he himself becoming a professional photographer, his brother David a schoolteacher and his sister Mamie the wife of a floor-walker in Robb's department store.

Self-portrait of Hogg in his mid-thirties, from one of his lantern slides.

After learning the druggist's trade in his uncle's business, Alex. Hogg was employed by the firm of Dobbin & Co., 'grocers, druggists and general merchants' as the 1894 directory describes them, where so far as we know he remained until he was thirty. During these years his interest in photography developed, and he became highly competent and well known as a leading amateur. The earliest of his photographs that has survived is of a scene on the river Lagan taken in 1888. We also have his photograph of the display in the 1894 Belfast Camera Club competition and a harbour scene dated 1895. A flashlight photograph of a meeting of the Ulster Photographic Society in November of the same year survives as a lantern slide. At this stage of his life Hogg seems to have been keenly interested both in experimenting with techniques - particularly flashlight photography - and also in trying to achieve 'artistic' effects.

During these years he also learned how to make lantern slides and became a keen lanternist. The Ulster Museum has the prize medal awarded to him by the Ulster Amateur Photographic Society in 1895 for lantern slides. In 1897 he delivered a prize 'lecturette' entitled 'By the Banks of Erne', illustrated by forty-six slides, before the Belfast Y.M.C.A. Camera Club. In those days forty-odd slides was nothing for the enthusiastic lecturer, or for his audience; Hogg himself used to deliver one which in its full form had over two hundred. His Y.M.C.A. lecturette was subsequently published in *The Amateur Photographer* with six illustrations. Its text gives us some insight into Hogg's interests and his approach to photography. He had a keen appreciation of natural beauty, which he expressed in somewhat trite and stilted language, and was also curious about the people he met. He found much on Lough Erne 'to make the landscape pleasing to the photographer with artistic taste', and recounted the conversation he and his two companions had with an old fisherman whose portrait they took. The highlight of the trip was an expedition to the underground caves at Boho: 'Having heard so much of

The title slide of Hogg's lecture on the river Lagan, which he used to deliver with more than two hundred illustrations.

the wonderful caves at Boho, seven miles away, we decided to visit them, and at the same time photograph them with the help of the flashlight. Taking the apparatus required, which included a Todd-Forret lamp, a Goertz W.A. lens and whole-plate camera, we set off on a jaunting car'. The local sergeant of police showed them the way to the caves (we still have the picture of him and his men standing outside their barracks). Armed with a supply of tallow dips, which were placed at intervals to guide them out, Hogg and his friends entered the caves and exposed several plates, having 'eventually succeeded in illuminating the caves with actinic rays equalling the sun itself', and thus obtained what Hogg claimed to be 'the only photographic records of these wonderful caves'. Other expeditions included one to the island of Devenish, past the ruins of Portora Castle, whose 'roofless weather-beaten towers, covered with the mosses of centuries, and mantled with ivy of the deepest green, form a

charming contrast to the grey old walls, and make it a tempting study for the photographer'.

By the time he was thirty, he was sufficiently absorbed in photography—and sufficiently confident in his skills—to give up the security of a regular salary for the uncertain career of a professional photographer. In 1900 there were already more than twenty photographic studios in the city, several of them employing large numbers of assistants. Most men of Hogg's age setting up on their own would have come from such an establishment and would have been able to advertise their professional competence by saying so, as one of them did in the 1890s by describing himself as 'late of Magill's'. Hogg took the plunge in 1901, when he started the studio in Trinity Street where he was to work for the next twenty years. His first appearance in the Belfast street directory was the following year, as 'photographic and lantern specialist'.

In 1907 he married Sara Marion Houston, a year his junior, who is said to have been a nurse at the Royal Victoria Hospital. They lived at first in a new house named 'Kineto' in Chichester Road, off the Antrim Road. The five houses which along with the police barracks on the corner made up this little street were all dignified with names: next door in 'Iona' lived a cashier named McKibben; across the street in 'Sunnyside' a grocer Owens, whose neighbour Crockett was an accountant, and in 'Fairview House' the widow Swanton. In 1912 the Hoggs moved to 10 Thorndale Avenue, where they lived for the next twenty years, until the first Mrs Hogg died in 1932. There is very little information about Sara Hogg, but she is remembered as a kind and likeable woman who looked after the business side of things. At some point she was knocked down in a street accident and injured severely enough to leave her with a pronounced limp. The Hoggs had no children.

In the 'Troubles' of the early 1920s Trinity Street, a mixed area of Catholics and Protestants, apparently became unsafe (we have a photograph of the jam factory nearby, on the corner with Clifton Street, burnt out by the I.R.A. in 1922). Hogg, by now one of Belfast's leading photographers, decided to move his business to the city centre when premises became

☐ *Hogg in his early thirties, a self-portrait.*

☐ *James Hogg's shop in York Street, Belfast, c.1903, where young Alex Hogg trained as a druggist. The business sold groceries as well as drugs, a common combination at the time: one window displays samples of tea and jam, the other Hogg's Cherry Balsam and Zulu Insect Destroying Powder. The photographer's next door, with its painted signboard showing a photographer at work, was not there during Hogg's time with his uncle.*

vacant on the top floor of 81 High Street, where there had been a studio for fifty years or more. Here he remained until after his first wife's death. On remarrying in 1934 he moved finally to 67 Great Victoria Street, where he both lived and worked until he died.

Hogg's second wife, Margaret Mann, whom he married when she was aged fifty-nine and he sixty-three, had worked for him for many years as a retoucher. She too had come to Belfast from the country, in her case from Glarryford in County Antrim. Her nieces recall that she was well-read and fond of quoting poetry, having intended to train as a teacher until a suspected weakness of the heart put an end to that (she lived to be eighty-seven!). She had learned retouching with the photographic firm of H. R. Hembry. Retouching was used extensively by all photographers throughout the period up to the Second World War, especially for portraits but also to give sharp definition to technical and commercial photographs.

A number of photographs of Hogg survive. The earliest, showing him in a dandified pose with his first moustache (a pale forerunner of the dashing affair he sported for most of his life) and wearing a braided jacket and watch chain, was taken at Abernethy's studio in High Street when the sitter was aged eighteen at most. Next is a self-portrait when he was thirty or so, about the time he became a professional photographer. A head-and-shoulders silhouette of 1925 was produced for use as a postcard. A fine half-plate portrait taken about 1930 is the best one of him in later life. He also appears in some of his own photographs of outings of amateur camera clubs in his early days, and later in groups of professional photographers in the 1920s and 1930s, and there is a clever self-portrait of him flat on his back on the floor of the City Hall photographing the dome. In later life he wore his hair rather longer than was usual at the time, in what those who remember him describe as an 'arty' style. This was an expression of a genuine if not particularly educated interest in art and artists: he was for many years an enthusiastic member of the Belfast Art Society (forerunner of the Ulster Academy of Arts) and of the Ulster Arts Club; and he always had yearnings to achieve 'artistic' pictorial effects when unconstrained by the mundane need to complete a bread-and-butter commission. His membership of the Arts Club, and of other organisations such as the Rotarians, reflected his convivial and gregarious nature. He was also a member of the orthodox presbyterian congregation in Rosemary Street, and had many contacts with church-based bodies such as the Y.M.C.A. and city missions.

Compared with, say, his distinguished friend and fellow photographer R.J. Welch, Hogg's intellectual interests appear to have been conventional. Nevertheless he had a genuine appreciation of Irish topography, natural history and archaeology, which led him to join the Belfast Naturalists' Field Club and the Belfast Natural History and Philosophical Society (and its Archaeological Section). The text of his lecture 'The River Lagan from Source to Sea', illustrated by over 200 of his own lantern slides, both shows the range of his interests and the limits of his talents as a commentator. By contrast with the rather uninspired commentary, the slides themselves showed his excellent eye for the informative and the picturesque. In his later years the Ulster Tourist Development Board gave him a commission he must have enjoyed, one which enabled him to express his love of the Ulster landscape in a series of superb pictures, equal in quality to Welch's famous views. Reports of his death in the local newspapers remarked that while his work covered every class of commercial and technical photography, he was best known for his views of Ulster beauty spots, which were used in numerous tourist and travel publications. They also noted that he had been 'a keen antiquary and naturalist, and devoted much of his spare time to photography in these spheres'.

During 1939 Hogg's health began to decline, and he died on 25 August. He was buried three days later in the City Cemetery on the Falls Road, in the plot which already contained the remains of his father, mother and first wife.

PROFESSIONAL
PHOTOGRAPHY
IN BELFAST BEFORE 1900

FOR ALL PRACTICAL PURPOSES, photography began in 1839. In August of that year Louis Daguerre published in Paris the process of fixing positive images on metal plates that was called after him. No sooner had the daguerreotype appeared than William Henry Fox Talbot announced the discovery of his own invention, Photogenic Drawing, which in 1841 he published and patented in improved form as the calotype or Talbotype, by which paper negative images could be transferred onto paper as positives. This was the basic idea of all subsequent photography for, unlike the daguerreotype which gave one, unique picture, the negative of the calotype could be printed again and again. News of these exciting developments quickly reached Belfast. The *Northern Whig* reported on 6 August 1840 that a local engraver, Francis Beatty, had made a 'photogenic drawing' of the Long Bridge. Beatty later claimed to have conducted experiments in photography for several years before this; certainly he appears to have been the pioneer of photography in Ireland. In 1842 he also opened the first photographic studio in Belfast, a year after the first in Ireland had been opened in Dublin. The first professional photographs taken in Belfast were Beatty's daguerrotypes. The earliest local photographic image to have survived, however, is from a calotype portrait of Belfast's resident landowner the second Marquis of Donegall, taken in 1843 and subsequently copied.

Technical complications, patents and licences—to say nothing of expense—restricted the use of daguerreotype and calotype during the decade after 1841. Then in 1851 Frederick Scott Archer, a sculptor who had taken up the calotype as an aid to his art, invented and published the process that was to make daguerreotype and calotype obsolete and to dominate photography for the next quarter of a century. This was the wet collodion or wet plate process. Archer declined to patent his invention, thus making it freely available to all and opening photography to a much greater number of people than ever before. In 1851 there were only fifty professional photographers in the whole of Britain. Ten years later there were more than 2,800. In Dublin, which had a dozen studios in the early 1850s, more than sixty new ones opened in the following decade. Belfast, with half-a-dozen by the end of the 1850s, had twice that number by 1864, and the total rose to fifteen in the 1870s. Everywhere, expansion was largely due to the growing popularity of the new portrait photography. Daguerreotype portraits, produced in the 1840s and early 50s, had been comparatively expensive and therefore almost entirely confined to the rich. The wet plate process made it possible for most people to afford

□ *The studio of the photographer H.R. Hembry in Donegall Place, Belfast. Hogg took this picture in 1921, when Hembry was giving up the premises, but it is a good illustration of what a late nineteenth century studio looked like.*

THE ROYAL ULSTER FINE ART STUDIO.

MACFARLAND BROS.
35. High St.
BELFAST

JAMES MAGILL
PHOTOGRAPHIC STUDIO
Donegall Place
BELFAST

COPIES AND ENLARGEMENTS TO ANY
SIZE MAY BE HAD FROM THIS NEGATIVE
BY SENDING THE NAME.

Marion, Imp. Paris

GIBSON'S
Portrait Studio
20. CASTLE LANE
BELFAST.
Plain & Coloured Portraits
Singly or in Groups.
VISITE PORTRAITS
6 Copies 8/ 12 Copies 12

J. MACK
PHOTO ARTIST
34. York Street
BELFAST

NEGATIVE PRESERVED
COPIES MAY BE HAD AT

a photograph of themselves, usually in the form known as a carte de visite (or by local photographers, less pretentiously, as a 'sticky-back').

The carte de visite—so called because its size and shape was that of the visiting cards used at the time—was responsible for an enormous increase in business for professional photographers. If the Frenchman André Disdéri was not actually its inventor, it was he who patented the process and it was certainly popularised by him. In England 'cartomania' broke out in 1860, after J. E. Mayall published his photographs of the royal family. By taking several small pictures on a single glass plate and developing the lot in one process photographers could supply photographs much more cheaply than before. When mounted on stiff card and covered with a protective varnish, these became very presentable—and durable. The famous flocked to be photographed, and thousands of these portraits were sold to people who for the first time were able to see what their rulers or heroes looked like. At the local level, sets of local celebrities were produced for sale. In 1865, Magill's were advertising cartes of 'the leading clergymen of Belfast and neighbourhood' at a shilling each.

Such was the demand that photographic studios sprang up in all sorts of premises, some of them pretty unlikely. Hairdressers, butchers, tobacconists, coffee sellers, even dentists opened or installed studios. The Belfast studio of Robert Galbraith, for example, made its appearance in 1868 first on the top floor of his 'Kephalolutron' (hairdressing establishment and baths) at 9 High Street, under the management of a Londoner named Payne Jennings, 'late Principal Operator at the Fine Arts Establishment of Mr Crawford [Cranfield], Dublin'. Here a gentleman could have his hair cut in the Private Room for a shilling, the price of a carte. At the bottom end of the market, cartes were sold for as little as sixpence each in 1865 by Alex. S. Mayne at his Ulster Tract, Book and Bible Depository in Donegall Square East.

One of the best-known and most successful of Belfast's early studios was that of James Magill. Like many studio owners of the period he started as something else, in his case as a stationer, in 1847. From the early

1850s his premises were at 2 Donegall Place; here he sold ordnance survey maps, distributed government stamps, sold paintings and prints, did gilding and frame-making, and cleaned and restored paintings. In 1861 he added a photographic studio, which flourished for the next thirty years. The large number of Magill's cartes which survive testify to the popularity of his portrait work among the solid citizens of Belfast. He also produced photographs of 'scenery, mansions, interesting historical ruins &c', few of which have survived.

The chief rival to Magill in the 1870s and 1880s was E. T. Church, whose establishment at 53 Donegall Place was opened in 1869. Church had learned his trade in London, with Henry Herring of Regent Street. Many of his cartes survive (including some done by R. J. Welch, who worked for him in the early 1880s) and he produced portraits on china and enamel, often finishing them in watercolour or oils. In 1891 he was claiming particular success for his new 'life sized oil portrait, which is mounted in broad gold frame, thirty by twenty-four inches, complete for £2.2s'. He claimed to photograph all sitters personally and to do all the colouring work himself, and boasted the patronage of H.R.H. Prince Arthur Patrick, Lord and Lady Dufferin,

Lord O'Neill and 'many of the local aristocracy and members of the highest circles of society in Belfast and the North of Ireland'. Church's name disappears from the directories after 1891. In the following year the studio at 53 Donegall Place was being run by W. J. Kilpatrick, a relative newcomer who had moved from no. 8 in the same street. According to his advertisements in 1892, Kilpatrick had visited the leading studios in the three kingdoms and had completely re-equipped the old Church studio, employing 'the greatest optician of the age' to construct for him a special set of lenses. He advertised portraits on porcelain (any size), carbon enlargements from carte to life size, ivory miniatures, platinotypes, outdoor photography, tennis, cricket, wedding and military groups. Interestingly, though, he gave special prominence to his 'portraits in oils up to life size on canvas (not coloured photos)', so he was evidently another of those 'artist photographers' who used both painting and photography in the production of portraits. Indeed, in the 1896 directory he appears simply as a portrait painter.

Also prominent was William Abernethy, who commenced business in 1886 at 29 High Street, where he occupied several floors. Like his rivals Church and Magill, he described his business in *Industries of Ireland* (London, 1891). His entry refers particularly to the handsome and tasteful surroundings, a studio forty-five feet long with all mod.cons. such as patent blinds and scenery on rollers, up-to-date apparatus such as a Meagher's patent camera with Dallmeyer lenses and instantaneous shutter, and 'one of the largest cameras in the kingdom for the new popular panel photos'. As well as every branch of photography, he supplied paintings in oil, water or black and white. The scale of his operations may be judged by the fact that he employed

▢ *Hogg (centre) and other members of the Y.M.C.A. Camera Club at Glenariff, County Antrim in 1898. Ten years earlier, the railway company which operated a narrow-gauge goods line between Ballymena and Parkmore had opened it to passenger traffic. Among other amenities the company provided for tourists was the rustic tea-house in the picture.*

'upwards of twenty experienced assistants' in the various departments, and he claimed, 'taking Saturday and Monday as average days', to photograph more than 300 clients a day.

■ *His hat at a stylish angle (he was something of a dandy in his younger days), Hogg is fourth from the left in the back row of this group of amateur photographers, c.1900. They are standing at the entrance to Newforge House, which overlooked a picturesque stretch of the river Lagan on the outskirts of Belfast.*

From the 1880s photography became a popular hobby for millions of people. The two inventions that brought this about were the development of the fast gelatine process or dry plate, which began to come into general use about 1880, following the discoveries of Dr R. M. Maddox, and Eastman's Kodak camera with a roll-film which was sent back to the factory for developing ('You press the button—we do the rest' was Eastman's fortune-making slogan). Amateur photographic societies were formed or revived. In Dublin the Photographic Society of Ireland, dormant since 1860, was reformed in 1879. In Belfast, where an earlier

society (started in 1857) had also foundered, the Ulster Amateur Photographic Society was established in 1885 and soon had a large number of members, one of whom was young Alex Hogg. With so many amateurs now able to produce good photographs easily, the years after 1880 in Dublin saw a marked decline in the number of photographic studios. This was not apparent in Belfast, where the number in 1880—sixteen—was only two fewer ten years later and thereafter rose steadily. The obvious explanation is the continuing phenomenal growth of Belfast's population as compared with that of Dublin.

Business in Belfast during the last twenty years of the nineteenth century was sufficient to attract several outside firms. In 1880 Thomas Williams & Co. of Plymouth opened a branch at 25 Castle Place. In the mid-eighties the Glasgow firm of Turnbull & Sons started at 23 Garfield Street. Turnbull's advertised their use of 'Patent Luxograph Apparatus' which enabled them to 'take photographs at all times and in all weathers, after dark as well as during the day' and were licensees for a number of patent processes. Unlike Williams, who had gone by 1884, Turnbull remained in Belfast for many years, till the end of the 1920s. Lafayette's, the great Dublin firm with branches in several British cities, opened in Donegall Place about 1900; it too remained until the end of the twenties.

Some local photographers exhibited and advertised at the Belfast art and industrial exhibition in 1895, held in the Linen Hall. The exhibitors included Abernethy, Hugh Adair (8a Donegall Place), William Benson (22 Lombard Street) Allison & Allison (14 Queen's Arcade, Donegall Place) and Robert Welch. Both Abernethy and the Allisons took full-page advertisements. Abernethy's mentions the gold medal awarded to him for his results in photographing children and also his large printing and finishing works on the outskirts of the city at Bloomfield, where 'the most skilled men are employed, so that the public may rely on first-class work, and not the hap-hazard results often tolerated by unskilled labour'. He also claims to have been honoured with over 18,000 sittings at his studios within the past year. It is clear that by the end of the century professional photography in Belfast was a thriving business.

PROFESSIONAL
PHOTOGRAPHER
1901 - 1939

WHEN ALEX HOGG opened for business as a professional photographer at 13 Trinity Street in 1901, there were already more than twenty studios in the city. The majority of them—and all of those dependent on the fashionable portrait trade—were to be found in the city centre, particularly in High Street and Donegall Place (each of which had five) and Royal Avenue. Not only was Hogg aiming to make his living in a field where competition was already pretty fierce, but his studio was far from the centre of things and unlikely to attract any passing trade. Trinity Street was a small street of only twenty houses off Clifton Street, directly opposite the Charitable Institution. It was inhabited at the turn of the century by a mixed population which included a couple of policemen, a foreman, a book-keeper, a tenter (supervisor of looms in a weaving shed), a china merchant, a chemist, a labourer, a carpenter, a house painter, a compositor and the proprietor of a public laundry. At number 3 lived the foreman, whose name was also Hogg. Number 5 was later occupied by William Hogg, a grocer. It seems likely that both 3 and 5, and perhaps the other five houses on that side of the street, belonged to Hogg's uncle Samuel, the prosperous Shankill Road grocer and provision merchant, and that the photographer started his professional career in Trinity Street because with few resources of his own he was glad to get whatever help he could from his relatives.

Unable at this stage of his career to compete to any great extent for the portrait trade, Hogg had to take whatever work he could find and make the most of the skills and contacts he had developed as an amateur. Two specialised areas, neither of which required an expensive studio and neither of which was overcrowded with professional rivals, suggested themselves: technical photography and lantern slides. From the beginning he described himself in the directories and in advertisements as 'photographic and lantern specialist'. One aspect of technical photography, the photographing of machinery, was to provide him with a good deal of his bread and butter during the next forty years. In the great industrial city that Belfast became during the late nineteenth century, with its shipyards, ropeworks, engineering works and linen mills, there was a growing number of such commissions, which required photographers to do their work on the spot rather than in the studio. As early as 1865 the photographer Massey was advertising the taking of views of 'public buildings, shop fronts, animals or machinery' though, to judge from most photographers' trade notices, machinery did not become a common subject until the end of the century, by which time technical advances in both photography and printing had made the reproduction of photographs for trade purposes easy and cheap. Abernethy (established 1886) advertised his ability to take views of buildings and machinery in much the same terms as Massey twenty years earlier. E. T. Church claimed to give special attention to photographing 'machinery etc. for trade purposes'. Both, however, depended for their success on portraiture. It was photographers not tied to studio work, such as R. J. Welch, who first picked up much of the new technical work. Welch was the official photographer for Harland and Wolff and went on all the trial trips of their great liners from 1896 until 1914. Hogg's senior by ten years and a professional photographer with a well-established reputation by the time the younger man set up in business, Robert Welch had already produced some first-rate photographs of machinery and industrial processes in the shipyards and linen mills of Belfast. He was best known, however, for work of a different kind, namely his pictures of Irish landcape, antiquities and folk customs. In the directories of the time he appears as the publisher of 'Irish views'.

It was to be some time before Hogg became a serious rival to Welch as a photographer of ships and linen: in both, his best work was done during the second half of his career. Between the wars he became official photographer to Belfast's other shipbuilders Workman Clark & Co. and also produced some outstanding pictures of the various processes by which linen was produced and marketed—pictures often more interesting than Welch's in that they show people at work rather than rows of unattended machines. From an early period, however, he became expert and sought-after as a photographer of the new electrical machinery, of the new electric trams in Belfast, and of motor vehicles. The earliest of his tramway pictures, dating from 1905, show the tracks for the electric trams being laid in the city centre. So far as motor cars are concerned, Hogg did not have the field entirely to himself—Welch and others also photographed the products of the Belfast firm of Chambers & Co. for example—but he seems to have done more work of this kind than anyone else, and to have added new clients as they appeared. Apart from Chambers & Co. (for whom he did a lot of work) his early list included such locally notable motor suppliers as Harry Ferguson, Charles Hurst, Leslie Porter, Victor H. Robb and J. B. Ferguson, not to mention commissions for vehicles owned by the Co-operative Society and other business firms. To these were later added such newcomers as Isaac Agnew, J. E. Coulter, and some of the private bus companies of the 1920s.

Specialising in the production of lantern slides enabled Hogg to turn to good account the many contacts he had established as an amateur. It was the age of the illustrated lecture and the magic lantern; indeed the three and a quarter-inch square lantern slide, by then standard, remained in universal use throughout Hogg's life and well beyond. As we have seen, he himself was a noted exponent of the illustrated public lecture. He also acted as official lanternist to the Field Club and the Natural History and Philosophical Society (his fee for the latter in the 1930s was a pound a lecture). He

Members of the Ulster branch of the Professional Photographers Association on an outing to Londonderry, 10 June 1932. The two figures at the back are Hogg and his friend R.J. Welch. Hogg was a keen promoter of the Association in his latter years and for a time in the 1930s served on its national council. The number of women in the party is interesting, though some may be wives of members rather than photographers themselves. Before the First World War professional photography was almost entirely a male preserve: only four studios run by women are listed in the Belfast directories between 1850 and 1914. More appeared during the emancipated twenties; in 1932 there were five in the city.

produced slides of his own photographs both for his own use and for sale, and also made slides from the photographs of Welch and other photographers. The A. R. Hogg Photographic Library, which is mentioned in

▢ *City of Belfast Camera Club's exhibition at the Y.M.C.A. in 1894. Hogg was a keen member of several amateur societies, and a frequent prizewinner.*

his negative register, was probably a collection of slides for hire. In fact, Hogg provided much the same service for Belfast and the north in the matter of slide illustrations as Thomas Mason, the Dame Street optician, did for Dublin and the rest of the country (Hogg's collection of slides includes a number of Mason's).

Some of the most interesting of Hogg's early photographs survive only as slides—the best of his pictures of slum housing scheduled for replacement under the Belfast Improvement Order of 1910; some of those of decayed National Schools in the city; rare pictures of the inmates of the Workhouse hospital; school playground games; the city's horse-drawn fire brigade and the laying of the electric tramlines; some striking studies of washerwomen and market traders.

Those in the Ulster Museum collection include a series on the history of photography—material for another of his lectures, possibly to an evening class at the College of Technology—and a number of the advertising slides he made for Belfast cinemas between the wars.

Another aspect of Hogg's career at this period, one about which we have no information except occasional mentions in advertisements, is cinematography. His first advertisement in the exhibition catalogue of the Belfast Art Society in 1902, the year in which he became a member, describes him as 'photographic, lantern and cinematograph specialist' and includes in his list of offerings 'animated photographic entertainments given in town or country'. In the years before the First World War he gave two regular weekly shows in Belfast. Not for nothing did he call his house in Chichester Road 'Kineto': the Kinetoscope was a type of cinematograph. Up to 1920 he continued to advertise moving picture exhibitions but thereafter—as commercial cinemas became more common—he appears to have given up.

Like any enterprising photographer, Hogg did a certain amount of uncommissioned work, either to market himself or in the hope of selling prints for publication. Many of these were views of the Irish countryside, particularly of the northern counties (though he travelled as far as Killarney in 1914). Even on his honeymoon in Donegal in 1907, he wrote to a cousin (on a postcard depicting a Lawrence view of Killybegs) that he was 'busy taking views for postcards'. He printed and marketed these himself in the early days, even in such out-of-the-way places as Swanlinbar, County Cavan, from which one surviving card was posted in 1905. Many of his views of the river Lagan turn up as postcards. Like any enterprising photographer, he photographed interesting events as they occurred. During the dockers' strike in Belfast in 1907, for example, he took a large number of pictures, including some which may well be the earliest of a Belfast riot mob in action, hurling stones at a detachment of the Cameronians on the Grosvenor Road. Whether he succeeded in selling any of these for publication is not known; he did, however, sell to *Commercial Motor* photographs of 'picket-proof motor wagons' used during the strike. He also photographed the public meetings, marches and parades associated with the Unionist opposition to Home Rule during the years before 1914, including the signing of the Solemn League and Covenant at the City Hall and the emergency hospital established in Clifton Street Orange Hall (just round the corner from his studio in Trinity Street) by the Ulster Volunteer Force.

Perhaps the best way to give an impression of Hogg's working life at this period is to look at the year 1912, the first for which we have something like a complete record in his register of negatives. By that date he was well established and must have been fairly prosperous, for the Hoggs moved in 1912 from the house in Chichester Road to a large three-storey terrace house in Thorndale Avenue, within walking distance of the studio in Trinity Street.

Though never primarily a portrait photographer, Hogg nevertheless had a considerable clientele once he became known, especially in the Antrim Road area where he lived and worked. Individuals he photographed in 1912 included Baby Scott and William Hogg, both of Trinity Street; Mr and Mrs Albert Hogg of Clanchattan Street; a city councillor named Clements; the minister of Duncairn Presbyterian Church and his family (an extraordinary number of pictures); a teacher at the School of Art at his easel, and a 'missionary to the jungle tribes'. Among the photographs of groups were a football team and gym groups from the Technical College (for which he did a great deal of work over the years); family gatherings, including the family of Harry Ferguson the inventor; a children's party (flashlight); the pupils of Hughes' Academy and St. Enoch's School; Y.M.C.A. groups; pupils of the Deaf and Dumb Institute in a performance of 'Oliver Twist' (flashlight); the annual social and outing of his old friends in the Chemists and Druggists Society; and one solitary wedding party.

That year he took views at Bangor, Donaghadee, Glenariff, Portstewart, Ardglass, Castledawson and Glaslough. He photographed the eclipse of the sun on 17 April, the launch of the *Oxfordshire* at the Queen's Island, several trams, a large number of motor cars and vans, some aeroplanes at Balmoral (where he also

recorded the great Unionist demonstration) and three of the new picture palaces, namely the Kelvin Picture Palace and New Princess Picture Palace in Belfast and the Picture House, Bangor. He had several commissions from the Works Department at the City Hall (including one of a David and Goliath encounter entered as 'Street accident between sweeping brush and car') and a considerable number from the City Surveyor. Solicitors provided him with a good deal of work in connection with ancient lights and accident cases. He was engaged by several architects to record buildings and sites, notably by the firm of Blackwood and Jury. Through these commissions he came to photograph many of Belfast's buildings, from the City Hall downwards; sometimes, as in 1912, this sort of work was done for new-style construction firms such as the Trussed Concrete Steel Co., Westminster or a roofing firm from Glasgow. Views of the convent and schools at Castleblayney, Co Monaghan were taken for

☐ *Trinity Street, Belfast in 1905. Number 13, where Hogg had his studio between 1901 and 1921, is the house nearest to the camera. Dating from the late 1860s and early 1870s, the houses in the picture are good examples of the respectable dwellings erected for the prosperous artisans and lower middle class of the expanding city. An urban motorway now runs through the site.*

an architect, as were those of Clonard Chapel in Belfast, but most photographs of churches—from Fisherwick Presbyterian Church to Sandy Row Mission Hall—were done for the church authorities. The Ulster Bank commissioned pictures of its branches at Mountpottinger in Belfast and at Ballyconnell, County Cavan. There were a few private houses, notably Castle Shane at Ardglass, which the Belfast solicitor and antiquarian F. J. Bigger had fitted up as a weekend and holiday retreat in what he conceived to be genuine Irish medieval style.

A considerable number of industrial buildings were also photographed by Hogg during 1912 : Ross Bros' damask factory at Bloomfield, Gallaher's tobacco factory in York Street, Oldpark Print Works, W. & S. Mercier's new mill at Laganview Street, Comber Distillery, Lambeg Bleach Works, the salt mines at Carrickfergus, Cantrell & Cochrane's mineral water works, the premises of City Skin and Hide. Commercial premises included several Co-operative Society buildings, Samuel Hogg's grocery and provision business on the Shankill Road, the Globe Tavern in Crown Entry, Dobbin's the druggists in North Street, Johnston's umbrella works and shop, butchers' and chemists' shops. Lastly, Hogg also recorded for advertising or similar purposes such things as window displays; furniture, paintings and maps; the work of classes in the Technicial College; priests' surplices, embroidered blouse fronts and other products of linen finishing firms, and linen damask designs (for Ross Bros).

During the First World War this pattern remained much the same. Many of the portraits were now of young men in uniform about to leave for the front or, later, copies made for their grieving parents; now too the first passport photographs appeared. Group portraits were sometimes of V.A.D. nurses, soldiers at camp at Ballykinlar and Newcastle, munitions workers, wounded soldiers convalescing or ladies working at the War Hospital Supply depot, as well as of the chemists and druggists on their annual outing. Photographs taken for motor firms now featured military ambulances as well as the usual civilian vehicles (the new 'Fergus' car was unveiled by J.B. Ferguson & Co. in November

1915). One peculiar local manifestation of the war effort recorded by Hogg was the cultivation of flax by volunteers on the golf course at Fortwilliam. On the whole, however, the photographer's life went on much as before, with commissions from architects, solicitors, business firms and the Corporation occupying most of his time.

The move from Trinity Street to High Street in 1921 brought Hogg a good deal more in the way of portrait photography. This was just as well, for it is clear from the records of the business that for a time in the early 1920s the postwar slump in trade restricted the industrial and commercial work on which his income largely depended. At about the same time the spread of the commercial cinema put an end to his moving picture shows. During the twenties membership of the Ulster Arts Club and the Rotary Club brought him a good deal of his portrait work, to judge from the large number of photographs that have survived of individuals and groups from both organisations. Through either the Arts Club or the Belfast Art Society, Hogg was closely acquainted with all the leading Ulster artists of his day, from the eccentric Robert Ponsonby Staples early in the century to Paul Henry and young William Conor later.

It is clear, however, from both his advertisements and his letter-heads between the wars, that he never regarded himself as primarily a portrait photographer. A letter-head of the early 1920s lists his particular activities as 'commercial, technical and industrial photography, lantern slides and enlargements'. A later one is more explicit, listing 'commercial, legal, textile, engineering, architectural and technical photography in all its branches'; the photographing of 'coloured objects, paintings, works of art' by panchromatic process; enlargements in 'Crayonite'—described as 'perfectly permanent pictures copied from any photograph and finished by expert artists' (what might be called a retouching tribute); 'lantern slides and the wants of lecturers'; 'high-class optical lantern exhibitions' and—rather interestingly—'printing, developing and enlarging for amateurs'. Not only for amateurs, as it happens: other professionals, notably Abernethy, appear in the accounts for work of this kind.

Business picked up again from the mid-twenties. New clients appeared. One such was the Belfast station of the British Broadcasting Company (there is a nice shot of the youthful Tyrone Guthrie with the cast of a radio play outside the Company's studio in Linenhall Street in 1925). The owners of many of the new cinemas that had put Hogg out of the movie business employed him to record their premises; he also made many of the slides they used to advertise their attractions. Changing times are also reflected in commissions from the Estates department of the Corporation (early council housing), in an increasing amount of work concerned with electricity, in pictures of food processing plants, and in work for such new-style public bodies as the Ulster Tourist Development Association. New sporting groups make their appearance too: Balmoral and Shandon Golf Clubs on the outskirts of the city, the Northern Bank ladies' hockey team (the 'Norstars'), and suburban tennis clubs.

A look at another year in his register is the best way of seeing how Hogg's photographic practice had changed. Twenty years on from 1912, in 1932, there were many more portraits and a great variety of groups (from a Shankill Road Mission gym team to an Italian Fascists' dinner). The amount of work done for lawyers and architects was much the same. Among architects, the firm of Blackwood and Jury was still prominent, but there were half a dozen others as well. The new Parliament at Stormont was prominent among the buildings photographed, along with the new Children's Hospital, new primary schools, a new hall for the Co-operative Society, several hotels and restaurants and a couple of cinemas. As in 1912, there was a considerable amount of work from the College of Technology. The window displays of Erskine Mayne's bookshop in Donegall Square were also recorded. William Ewart & Son employed Hogg to photograph a display of their Irish linens, some machine drawings and an accident in their mill. He photographed machinery at several other mills, and took pictures of work in Gallaher's tobacco factory (and of William Gallaher's house in Malone Park).

Vehicles photographed during the year included motor cars (an M.G. Midget, for example), vans (the fleet of the Globe Laundry), trams, buses and petrol tankers. New traffic signals and concrete roadways were allied subjects. Among the shops of the new age was the General Electric Company's showroom. A demonstration of the new fashion in women's hairstyling, permanent waving, was photographed at the Carlton; so was the totalisator at Dunmore Park greyhound track. Agricultural photographs were taken at a government research station and two agricultural colleges, and various superior animals had their pictures taken at the Balmoral showgrounds. The only prominent public event recorded was the visit of the Prince of Wales. Many paintings, statues and art objects were photographed for the Museum and Art Gallery, as well as mosaics in Belfast Cathedral. As always, Hogg took a number of uncommissioned views—rather fewer than usual that year, it seems—at Bangor, Kilkeel and Downpatrick, as well as several of the Albert Memorial, that well-known landmark just outside his studio in High Street.

THE
PHOTOGRAPHS

THE YEAR after Hogg's death, his widow sold the studio in Great Victoria Street as a going concern, along with his stock of negatives. The purchaser, Seymour Hicks, had started his career in England as an employee of Lafayette's before coming to Dublin to work as a portrait photographer in the famous Werner studio in Grafton Street, where he eventually took over the business. A considerable number of Hogg's early negatives had been disposed of by Hogg himself at the time of his move from Trinity Street to High Street and more may have gone later, when he moved finally to Great Victoria Street. According to the recollection of the new owner's daughter, however, a large number of boxes containing the Hogg collection were properly stored in good conditions in the return of the building.

During the years that followed, Hicks produced prints from Hogg's negatives as requested by customers— transport history enthusiasts, for example. His main business was portraiture, however, and the Hogg collection inevitably suffered from neglect. Worse, the roof of the room in which it was stored was damaged in a storm and not repaired for some time, with the result that thousands of plates were ruined before the rest could be removed to better quarters. When Hicks died, his daughter carried on the business for a time before disposing of the remaining contents of the studio to the Ulster Museum in 1968.

Despite the loss or destruction of so many of his negatives, a substantial sample of Hogg's work has survived. The photographic prints in the Public Record Office of Northern Ireland include many of the pictures he took for Belfast Tramways, while the College of Technology has an interesting collection of his prints depicting the College and its activities. The collection in the Ulster Museum—from which all the pictures printed in this book are taken—consists of some 5,500 glass negatives (mostly full plate size), about 1,500 glass lantern slides and several hundred prints. The Museum also acquired Hogg's register of negatives. Recently Miss Hicks has kindly donated the account books of the studio from the early 1920s onward; taken along with the register these provide valuable information about the nature and scale of Hogg's photographic practice. The negatives themselves usually contain the name of the client and the date, as well as negative and box numbers corresponding to those in the register. Indeed Hogg was as thoroughly professional in the organisation and record-keeping side of his business as he was in taking photographs.

Hogg used a ten-colour card index of subjects, which is a useful guide to what he himself saw as the best arrangement of his extremely varied output. Portraits and groups formed one category, landscapes and views another. Buildings, shop windows, streets, street scenes and work done for surveyors, lawyers and architects were another. Artistic subjects such as paintings, jewellery, stained glass and musical instruments were lumped together. So too were machinery, ironwork, motor cars, aeroplanes and engineering; catalogue work and goods samples; sculpture, monuments and graves; timber yards, ships, launches and lighthouses; animals, dairy supplies, natural history and bees (perhaps he had cause to remember the bees). His last category consisted of the A. R. Hogg Photographic Library and material relating to customers and business houses. The arrangement of the photographs in this volume is loosely based upon Hogg's own system, with some emphasis on the subjects in which the Ulster Museum collection is particularly strong. The most important divergence is the inclusion of a section entitled 'People at Work', drawn from several of his categories. This section is based on hindsight rather than on Hogg. Taken along with some of the other photographs, most obviously those of linen workers, it illustrates the potential of the collection as a source of information about the working lives of Ulster people over a period of four decades.

The extraordinary historical interest of these photographs arises in part from the fact that Hogg was, most of the time, an ordinary professional photographer. By this I mean that he did what he was commissioned by clients to do, for everyday purposes, rather than consciously recording what he himself thought might be of interest to posterity. He was by no means an ordinary photographer in any other sense. Most of his local contemporaries whose names are still recalled—Abernethy for example—specialised in portraits. Hogg could hold his own with any of them, though portraits were only a small proportion of his work. No contemporary produced better landscapes and views either. His pictures of the City Hall and other Belfast buildings shows that he had no superior as an architectural photographer. Those of machinery and of the processes by which linen was manufactured, whether purely technical or more generally descriptive in character, equally justified his claims to expertise in such matters. In fact, with the exception of R. J. Welch, none of Alex Hogg's contemporaries in Ireland rivalled his achievement—an achievement in no way diminished by the fact that he lived and worked in one provincial city all his life. Indeed, the high quality of his work in such a varied range of subjects can have been matched by few photographers anywhere. It is this that makes him as remarkable in retrospect as it made him professionally respected in his own day.

Hogg (right), then aged sixty-one, and some of his cronies from the Ulster Arts Club at a dinner in the Carlton Restaurant, 15 August 1931.

PLACES

HOGG PHOTOGRAPHED the Irish—and especially the Ulster—landscape all his life. In fact, his earliest surviving photograph, dated 1888 when he was seventeen or eighteen, is of a scene along the river Lagan; and like any amateur, then or since, he spent much of his time in his early days recording views. Some of these pictures were sufficiently good to be included in the collection of the National Photographic Record Association, the body founded in 1897 by Sir Benjamin Stone 'to show those who will follow us, not only our buildings, but our everyday life, our manners and our customs'. Hogg was awarded the Association's gold medal, for photographs such as those he took in the Boyne valley at the turn of the century. Many of his best early views were taken during outings with the Belfast Naturalists' Field Club or the Belfast Art Society. Later he produced some fine work of this kind for the Northern Ireland Tourist Development Board.

Harvesting near Castlewellan, County Down in the 1920s, with the Mourne mountains in the background.

The harbour at Ardglass, County Down in the 1930s. During the Middle Ages, Ardglass was an important small port, defended by several castles, one of which can be seen in the background. In more recent times it became a centre for the herring trade of the Irish Sea, handling the catches not only of the local fleet but also of boats from many other ports.

■ Entrance to the prehistoric burial mound at Newgrange, County Meath, c.1900, one of a number of interesting pictures taken by Hogg during an extensive tour of the Boyne valley and reproduced when he became a professional photographer. These included a flashlight shot of the interior of Newgrange, looking up at the capstone, which he described as 'a rare photograph' but which survives only as a faded print.

High cross at Donaghmore, County
Tyrone c.1905. Donaghmore (Big Church) was
the site of an early monastery, of which this
cross, sixteen feet high and finely carved, alone
survived.

Cutting the corn at Lisnalinchy, near Ballyclare in County Antrim, c.1904. The farmer Isaac Montgomery and his son are on the reaper, his two daughters are tying the sheaves, and two other helpers are raking and gleaning. The girl in the white blouse became Mrs Hagan in 1905, an event which has enabled her daughter to date the photograph.

Cushendall, County Antrim, c.1910, with the distinctive shape of Lurigethan mountain in the background. The glens of Antrim were much visited by antiquarians and tourists, most of whom at this date would have travelled around the area by jaunting car.

Cloister of Sligo Abbey, an early (undated) photograph. Strictly speaking a Dominican friary, the abbey was founded in 1253 and added to at various times up to the fifteenth century.

Secular cloister: the brickworks at Killough, County Down, 2 September 1914.

■ Church Street, Bangor, County Down, 18 June 1903, with the Abbey Church in the background. Like all Belfast photographers, Hogg took a great many views of Bangor, which was a favourite place of resort for city-dwellers— and easily reached by road, rail or water. Unlike most views of the place, this one shows the ordinary town rather than the popular seafront and harbour.

Selling eggs on market day in Aughnacloy, County Tyrone in 1914.

 View of Slemish mountain, County Antrim, c.1907.

 Glenoe, County Antrim, 23 June 1906. Close to Larne and within easy reach of Belfast, this hamlet in a wooded glen with a waterfall was much visited—and much photographed—by lovers of the picturesque. Hogg took this picture for a postcard view.

The inn at Bryansford, County Down, just opposite the back gate of
Tollymore Park, the home of Lord Roden. The date of the photograph is
uncertain, but it was probably taken shortly before the First World War.
Tollymore Park is now a popular forest park and the inn a dwelling house.

The old castle at Crom, near Newtownbutler in County Fermanagh, an undated photograph. Built in the early seventeenth century, the castle was successfully defended against the Jacobites in 1689 by Abraham Crichton, ancestor of the earls of Erne whose modern mansion stands nearby.

■ Castle Upton, Templepatrick, County Antrim. The date is uncertain but probably c.1914.

Stormont Castle, County Down, March 1915. Taken by Hogg during a Field Club outing, this photograph shows the castle (built in the 1830s but towered and turretted later) as it looked before the British government bought it from the Cleland family and presented it to the new government of Northern Ireland as the prime minister's official residence.

LINEN

UNLIKE ITS OTHER two notable
recorders, R.J. Welch and W.A. Green,
Hogg took only a few photographs of the
rural and domestic aspects of the linen
manufacture. Most of his pictures illustrate
the factory processes of preparing and
spinning the yarn and of weaving,
bleaching and finishing the cloth. The bulk
of the surviving photographs date from the
1920s and 1930s, but there are also some
interesting earlier ones which Hogg
himself preserved and included in a later
series—a sign that the industry was
beginning to be seen as having had its
golden age. In fact at one point in 1938
orders for linen had declined so much that
56 per cent of the workforce was
unemployed. The Second World War led to
a (temporary) revival.

❏ Jacquard looms weaving linen damask,
c.1900. The weavers worked in very cramped
conditions.

The Jennymount mill of Philip Johnston & Sons, flaxspinners, North Derby Street, Belfast, c.1905. The houses in the street were inhabited by 'spinning masters' and labourers.

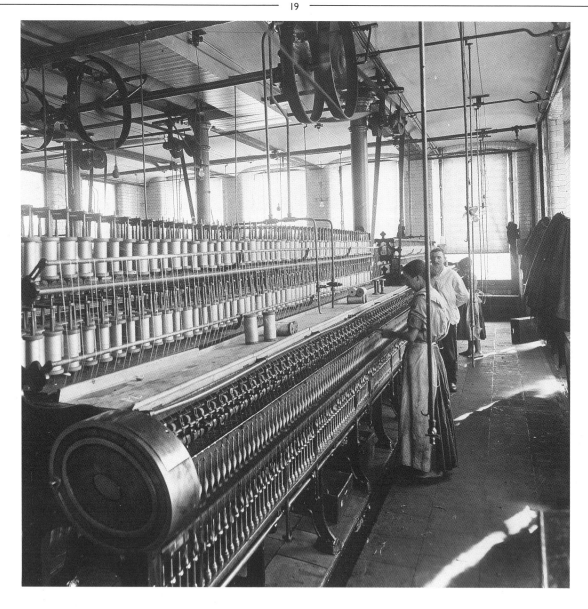

Spinning in a Belfast linen factory, c.1910. The two women in the picture are barefoot: on the wet, slippery floor this was safer than being shod.

A winding room in the 1930s, where hanks of yarn were wound onto spools or bobbins ready for warping. The girls on the left are straightening hanks on the 'poles', before placing them on the 'swifts' (skeleton wheels).

■ Rippling flax, undated. The heads of the plants were drawn through toothed combs of the kind shown on the right, thus removing the seed bolls.

■ Damask designer at work at Old Bleach, Randalstown, Co. Antrim. Most large firms employed their own designers, some of whom were successful artists in their own right. They worked on the premises and their designs were jealously guarded as trade secrets. From the squared paper, the designs were transferred to the jacquard punched cards which automatically controlled the pattern produced by the loom.

Another early photograph of jacquard looms at work in a Belfast weaving shed. The swags of punched cards carrying the pattern can be clearly seen.

Jacquard looms at Brookfield factory,
Cambrai Street, 16 September 1937.

A plain linen loom, without the elaborate superstructure of the jacquard attachment, at Brookfield Linen Co.'s mill on the Crumlin Road, May 1911.

◻ Chemical bleaching of linen, sometime between the wars. One of the 'kiers' or boiling vats can be seen open on the right. Before 1939 most good-quality linen was grass-bleached or at least finished on grass.

Laying out linen for bleaching in the open air at the Old Bleach works, Randalstown, County Antrim. The picture is from an album of prints done for the firm in the 1930s. Photographs of bleachgreens are not uncommon, but it is characteristic of Hogg to make an interesting composition of this workaday scene.

'Beetling' linen in an Ulster mill in the 1930s. The heavy wooden beetles pounded the surface of the cloth as it revolved, giving it fullness and a characteristic sheen. Deafness was almost inevitable for beetlers; the continuous rumble of a beetling mill in operation could be heard a long way in country areas.

Inspecting and folding linen in the warehouse. The photograph was taken in 1925. Webs were passed over the rails in front of the windows for a close inspection of the fabric, by workers called (as such workers still are) cloth passers.

The packing room at Leacock & Co.,
Linenhall Street, February 1934.

 Exterior of the Embroidery School, Maghera, County Londonderry, 1913. According to the entry for Maghera in the 1912 directory, 'A factory for making embroidery and other fancy work is in course of erection for Messrs. Glendinning, McLeish & Co., Belfast, and will employ several hundred hands'. It was employing about one hundred in the 1920s. Hogg took his pictures of the place shortly after it opened in 1913.

 Interior of the Embroidery School at Maghera in 1913. The machines produced what is known as Swiss embroidery, used particularly for handkerchiefs. The machines in the picture were in fact of Swiss manufacture, made by Georg Baum of Rorschach, though the operator's stool looks like a piece of local ingenuity. By means of a pantograph he is embroidering the master design (at one-sixth of its size) on the fabric. Since the machine turned out batches of thirteen dozen, mistakes were expensive—hence the need for special training.

Showroom of Samuel Lamont & Co., 10 Linenhall Street, 23 November 1937.

Old Bleach cut-work tea-table linen, photographed for an advertisement.

PEOPLE AT WORK

OTHER SECTIONS of this book—notably the one on linen—contain photographs that show people at work. The range of choice is so wide, however, that it seemed a pity not to devise a special selection with that theme. As it happens, there are several sets of unusual occupational pictures to choose from: for example, two laundries are recorded in great detail, and also the activities of workers in the bottling plant of Lyle & Kinahan's. Perhaps the most striking pictures are those taken for the Workshops for the Blind. It would not have been difficult to make a quite different selection.

■ Aristocrats of the outfitting trade: the cutting room staff of Messrs W.J. Marshall, tailors, 37 High Street, Belfast, 7 February 1931.

■ The other end of the business: the sewing room at Marshall's with workers—all men—in traditional posture and close to the daylight.

 Belfast washerwoman, c.1905, one of a number of similar studies of working women that Hogg made into lantern slides.

Market trader, c.1905, another lantern slide.

■ The office of the Monarch Laundry, Donegall Road, Belfast, 13 May 1936.
The bare floor, tongue-and-groove walls and hard chairs (too low for some of
the girls, who are perched on piles of ledgers) were typical of many business
offices of the period.

Draughtsmen at work in the drawing office of the Belfast Corporation electricity department, East Bridge Street, in 1938.

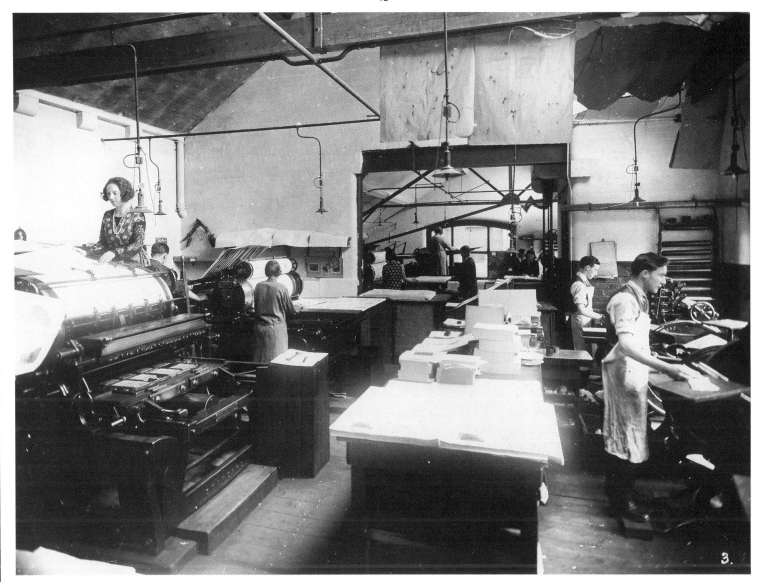

❏ Women workers ironing shirts at the Devonshire Laundry, Ravenhill Avenue, Belfast in February 1931. Note the makeshift basket stands, the collarless shirts and the workers' efforts to brighten their cheerless quarters with pinups of film stars. One Belfast laundry—perhaps one in every city—used to proclaim: 'Dirty collars are not becoming to you—they should be coming to us'.

❏ Workers in the printing and stationery firm .of Graham & Heslip, Franklin Street, Belfast in October 1930.

 Electricity Board workers with a petrol-driven boring machine, somewhere in County Armagh on 17 November 1931.

Employees playing tennis at Newforge, 2 August 1937. The owner of Newforge Ltd, Clement Wilson, came to Belfast from Scotland in 1928 and bought a derelict factory at Malone for his animal by-products business. In 1936 he transferred this offensive trade to a new site near Lisburn. Thereafter the Newforge premises, with the modern additions seen here, were used to produce only edible food products. Partly in order to counter local prejudice—but also from a genuine, and unusual, belief in the importance of a beautiful environment for his employees—he surrounded the factory with parks and gardens. After his death in 1975 the grounds were acquired by the city council for use as a public park, now named after him.

Workers and Corporation officials at the municipal abattoir, McAuley Street, in 1901. The superior status of the clerk on the right is clearly indicated by his clothing. This was Belfast's first public slaughterhouse, built in 1869 on the model of the one in Paris—Europe's finest—and later enlarged. By the end of the century it was quite inadequate, but it took seventeen years of debate and controversy—and a tour of Europe by a deputation of councillors—before a new one was opened in 1913. In 1870 the number of animals slaughtered here was 1,050; the new abattoir dealt with 82,395 in the year 1913-14.

Smithy work at the Columnar Basalt Co., Portrush, County Antrim. Some touches of modernity, such as the electrically-operated blower (evidently the reason for taking the picture) should help in dating what is still a largely traditional scene of activity. In fact, Hogg took this photograph on 20 June 1937.

 Women workers in primitive conditions, boxes balanced on knees,
separating tobacco leaf in Gallaher's factory in York Street, Belfast, 29 January
1932.

The clean end of the tobacco manufacturing business: girls packing cigarettes at Gallaher's York Street factory, 4 July 1932.

The patriarchal figure of Joseph Forde, weaving coarse matting in the Workshops for the Industrious Blind, Lawnbrook Avenue, Belfast. The photograph was taken in 1937 and subsequently published in the *Radio Times* in connection with a national appeal for the blind. Other photographs taken on the same occasion show blind workers weaving baskets, making brushes and stuffing mattresses.

Dental mechanics at McCallister's, 32 Wellington Place, Belfast in September 1929 making false teeth. The mug shots on the chart by the window illustrate different shapes of face and jaw, though it is not clear how such a general classification would help in producing dentures for an individual. The freckled lad in short trousers must have been straight out of school.

Packing bottles at Lyle & Kinahan's, Cullingtree Road, Belfast in the 1920s.
One of the leading wine and spirit merchants and ale bottlers in the city, Lyle &
Kinahan's also manufactured aerated waters (Belfast was notable for the purity
of its springs), and had an artesian well 250 feet beneath their premises.

The man from the ministry—in this case the Department of Agriculture—inspecting samples of potatoes going for export, at the Belfast docks on 11 January 1938. Though unable to do much to halt the decline of shipbuilding and linen, the government of Northern Ireland between the wars led the rest of the British Isles in improving agricultural produce and marketing. Among other produce, potatoes were subject to a compulsory marketing scheme which ensured minimum standards.

HARBOUR AND SHIPS

THROUGHOUT HOGG'S LIFE, the shipyard was the largest single employer of labour in Belfast, and its fluctuating fortunes had a correspondingly large effect on the local economy. Hogg took many photographs both of the shipyard and of the harbour area. Launches of ships such as *Titanic* and *Olympic* were great public occasions, and were recorded not only by Harland & Wolff's official photographer R.J. Welch but also on a freelance basis by Hogg and others—hence the close similarity of some of these pictures to Welch's photographs of the same scenes. As well as being employed by the shipbuilding firm of Workman, Clark & Co., Hogg received frequent commissions from the Harbour Board, so there are a large number of photographs of ships and harbour scenes in the collection.

Shipyard workers leaving Harland & Wolff's yard at Queen's Island in April 1914. At that time the yard employed some 14,000 workers, and special trams were laid on to cope with the crowds that streamed out at the end of a shift.

■ The launch of the *City of Sydney* at Workman, Clark's yard, 2 October 1929. The picture is a good example of Hogg's ability to compose an interesting scene. Hogg was official photographer to the firm between 1928 and 1935 (when it went out of business). *City of Sydney* was one of a number of cargo ships built for Ellerman Lines.

Belfast harbour scene, c.1902. The tug in the foreground is pulling barges laden with coal for the gasworks upstream.

The great floating crane at Queen's Island, October 1908. The technological modernity of the 200-ton monster, the largest in the world at that time, contrasts oddly with the traditional appearance of the sailing ship and the old-fashioned hoist on the quayside.

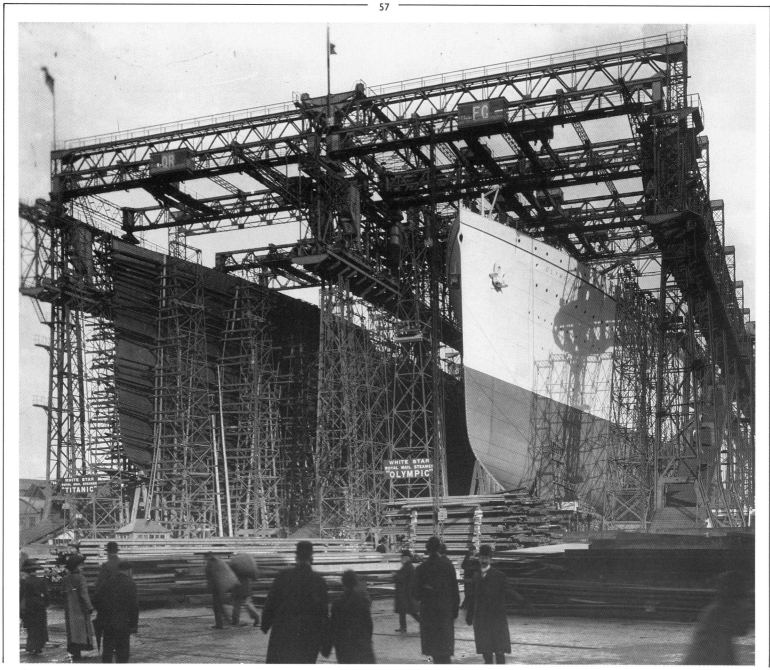

❑ *Titanic* and *Olympic* together in the slips at Harland & Wolff's yard in 1910. *Olympic* is painted and almost ready for launching.

❑ The launch of the *Olympic*, 20 October 1910. Before she was withdrawn from service she had made 257 round crossings of the Atlantic.

■ The launch of R.M.S. *Titanic*, 13 May 1911, at Harland & Wolff's yard at Queen's Island. The firm had been building progressively larger passenger liners for the White Star Line, for use on the North Atlantic run. *Titanic* was the largest and finest of all. Its launch was to be the high point of the yard's fortunes.

■ The memorial to the Belfast victims of the *Titanic* disaster. When the great liner struck an iceberg on her maiden voyage and went down with the loss of 1,500 lives, Belfast was stunned. This picture shows the memorial as it looked when first erected in the roadway in Donegall Square North, before it was moved to its present position in the grounds of the City Hall.

Laying electric cable across Belfast harbour, August 1934.

Royal Navy ships moored at Pollock Dock, 11 June 1934, with Rank's flour mills across the water.

❏ Loading potatoes for export at the Clarendon docks, 13 January 1938.

❏ The launch of the concrete ship *Creteforge* at Warrenpoint, County Down, 3 March 1919. The pictures of the launch were commissioned by the makers, J. & R. Thompson, Roden Street, Belfast, a firm of builders specialising in reinforced concrete construction. *Creteforge* was one of a number of concrete vessels ordered by the Shipping Controller towards the end of the First World War. Twelve ocean-going tugs and about fifty barges, all with names beginning with *Crete*, were built. The *Creteforge* was one of the barges. Entered in Lloyd's register of sailing ships for 1920-21 at 712 tons and registered in London, it was licensed for the coasting trade.

TRANSPORT AND TRAVEL

FROM THE EVIDENCE of his register, Hogg's studio at the time of his death must have contained a large number of negatives recording changes in transport over the preceding forty years. Unfortunately, many have not survived, including most of those he took for local motor manufacturers such as Chambers Bros. Fortunately, however, some of those that do remain are unusually interesting—such as a group of lantern slides recording the re-laying of the tramlines in Belfast in 1905, and a slide of Ferguson's aeroplane five years later. Hogg's professional career began at a time when most of Belfast's traffic—including its trams and its fire engines—were still horse-drawn. By the time of his death, scheduled air services carrying passengers and mail between Belfast and the principal cities in Britain were well established. Among his later photographs, in fact, are some of the new Belfast Airport at Sydenham.

Rural incident: a collision between Mr H. McNeill and Father Blacker near Cushendun, County Antrim, 2 May 1929. Hogg was sent from Belfast by a firm of solicitors to take this photograph. Since both vehicles appear to be undamaged, it looks as if the owners had agreed to reconstruct the encounter for his benefit. The car on the left is a Model T Ford.

Mr Johnston's petrol station at Carryduff, County Down, 22 May 1933. Here you could be sure not only of Shell but also of B.P., M.S. [Munster Simms], Mobiloil and Crown. If your car failed you, you could consult the Belfast Omnibus Company's timetable for the next bus to Belfast, Downpatrick or Ballynahinch.

☐ Horse-drawn trams in Donegall Place, c.1902, from a lantern slide. These vehicles, and the first electric trams which replaced them (fifty of which were older ones converted) were open on top. In a city of horses, the sweeper—the main subject of the picture—was an essential public servant. Though much else has changed in the street, Mullan's bookshop is still there.

Laying lines for the electric tramway in 1905, one of a number of lantern slides of this interesting operation. The elaborate junction shown here was at the corner of York Street and Donegall Street.

◻ Silver Jubilee tram, 10 May 1935. The early open-topped vehicles, such as this conversion of a horse-drawn tram, remained in use. Despite the exhortations of his loyal subjects, George V did not live much longer.

Horse-drawn ambulance operated by Belfast Fire Brigade, 1910 or earlier, from a lantern slide. Belfast was the pioneer in combining fire and ambulance services, a system followed by most other cities in the British Isles until the 1940s and still in operation in Dublin.

◻ The Belfast and County Down Railway terminus at Queen's Quay, at 12.9p.m. precisely on 19 April 1913. Trams ran directly to and from the station yard, as the lines going right show. There is only one motor vehicle in sight.

Interior of the Belfast and County Down Railway terminus at Queen's Quay,
5.17 p.m., 2 June 1933.

 Horse-drawn delivery vans of the Globe Laundry, Falls Road, July 1932.

The Globe Laundry's fleet of motor vans, July 1932.

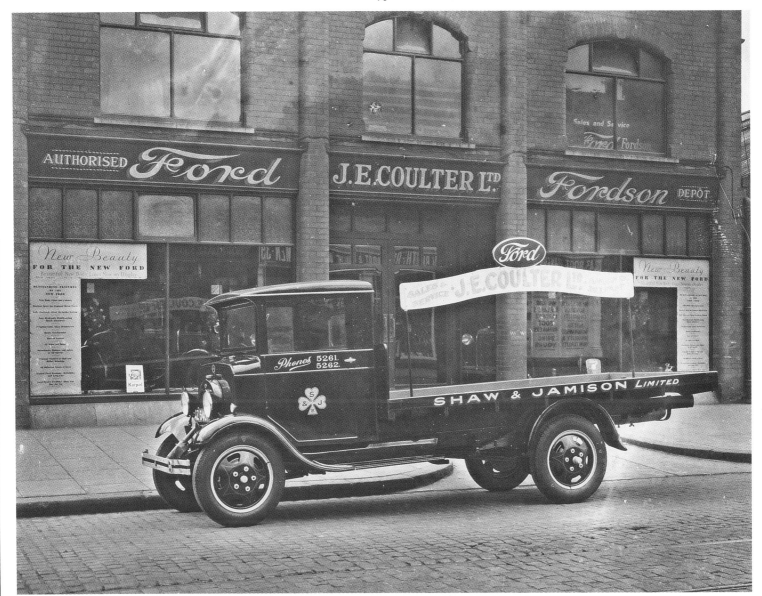

■ Mr Pyper, manager of Wood Milne's tyre depot in Donegall Square West, in his firm's splendid Napier car in Victoria Square, Belfast, 2 March 1918.

■ J.E. Coulter's premises at 50-56 Antrim Road, Belfast, June 1930, with a Fordson vehicle for Shaw & Jamison Ltd., a firm of wholesale chemists and druggists in Townhall Street. Coulter's was one of the new motor firms that Hogg acquired as a client in the 1920s.

■ Harry Ferguson and his aeroplane at Donard demesne, Newcastle, County Down in July 1910. Ferguson took the plane to Newcastle on 15 July in order to put on a flying display the following week. After several attempts to get airborne at Newcastle itself had failed, he took off successfully from Dundrum Bay on 8 August, flew over the town and landed in front of the Slieve Donard Hotel, winning a prize of £100 for the feat. In this picture the aeroplane still has the wooden struts used to secure it on its road trailer.

■ Belfast Harbour Airport, Sydenham, 15 December 1937. The new airport, built by the aircraft construction firm of Short Bros & Harland on land reclaimed from Belfast Lough, was officially opened by Mrs Neville Chamberlain on 16 March 1938. The civil airlines which had been using the airfield at Newtownards transferred to this one, which was five minutes' drive from the city centre. An earlier, unsuccessful venture, at Balmoral on the south side of the city, had been the first municipal airport in the United Kingdom when it was opened in 1924.

HEALTH AND WELFARE

SEVERAL SECTIONS of this book—notably those dealing with housing and education—contain photographs which give glimpses of the deplorable social problems that existed in Belfast alongside its prosperity. In addition to slum houses and slum schools, the Hogg collection includes extremely interesting photographs of hospitals and welfare establishments. Some, such as his pictures of the pauper inmates of the Workhouse and its infirmary, are unique. Hogg seems to have had good connections with medical people and officials concerned with charity and welfare work; some were members of organisations to which he too belonged. He also had a wide acquaintance among clergy involved in dealing with the poor.

Despite its rather patronising caption, 'Having our picture took', this lantern slide gives a real glimpse of the dirt and deprivation of Belfast's poor children in the early 1900s.

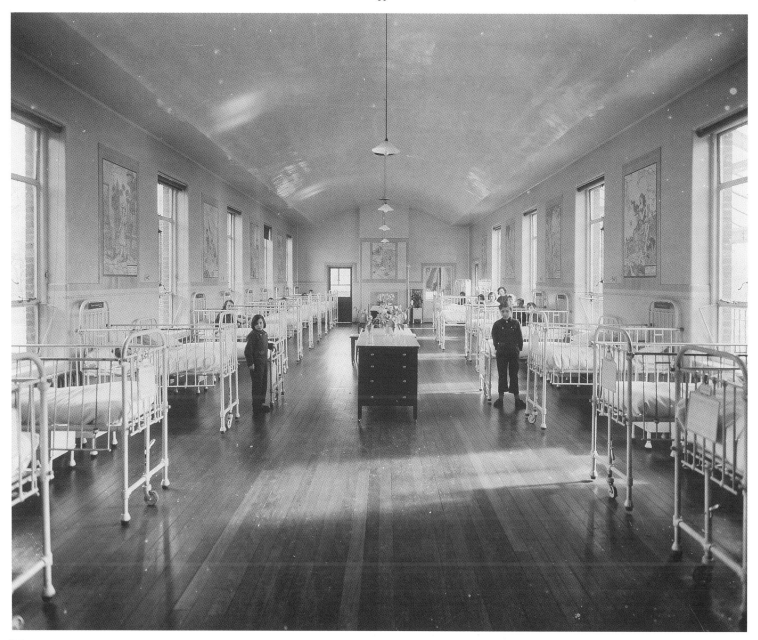

A ward in the new Hospital for Sick Children, Falls Road, 29 March 1933.

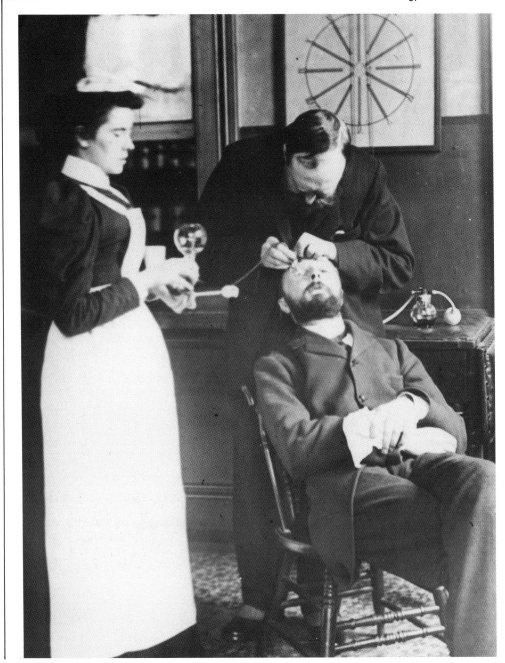

◼ Eye operation at the Benn Hospital, Clifton Street, Belfast, c.1902, from a lantern slide. The doctor is almost certainly William Alexander McKeown, the hospital's first surgeon (and first lecturer in ophthalmology at Queen's College). McKeown had an international reputation, especially for his successful use of an electro-magnet to remove metal fragments from the inner eye—an operation he first performed on a shipyard apprentice in 1874. His controversial views on education, and his employment of Hogg in that connection, are mentioned elsewhere.

 Cookery section of the Ulster Volunteer Force emergency hospital in the
Orange Hall, Clifton Street, Belfast, c. 1913. From 1912 thousands of unionist
women enrolled as part-time nurses, and emergency hospitals such as this one
were established as part of the preparations to resist Home Rule. The Orange
Hall in Clifton Street was just around the corner from Hogg's studio.

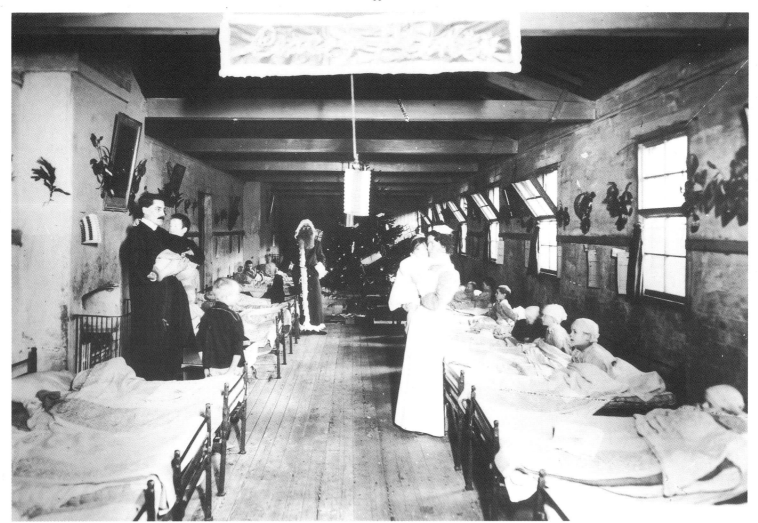

☐ Christmas Day in the Workhouse: a children's ward in the Belfast Union Infirmary, c.1906, from a lantern slide. Visiting medical staff in June 1900 reported unfavourably on the accommodation: 'The Children's Infirmary is in an unsatisfactory state; there are between 115 and 160 cases and only room for 90'. In 1905 the Belfast Board of Guardians decided to build a new Children's Infirmary, which opened in 1909. As this photograph shows, the old one was both crowded and spartan. The staff evidently did their best to bring Christmas cheer, with Santa Claus (the Rasputin-like figure in the background) and decorations.

The Intercepting Hospital, West Twin Island, Belfast harbour c.1910, from a lantern slide. In 1873 the Board of Guardians erected a single hut on this deserted spot to deal with an expected outbreak of cholera. Other huts were added in 1884 and 1892 and again in 1900 (when there was plague in Glasgow). The hospital never had any cholera cases, but it was used for smallpox patients on several occasions. In 1910, by which time they were interfering with the development of the harbour, these buildings were burned down by the Fire Brigade and the hospital moved to another site. No other picture of it is known to exist.

■ Another piece of medical history: men's pavilion, Abbey Sanatorium, Whiteabbey, County Antrim c.1910. In 1904 the Belfast Board of Guardians bought the former home of the Lanyon family as an auxiliary workhouse for the treatment of pulmonary tuberculosis. Four pavilions and a hospital were built in the grounds, the house itself being used by medical staff and nurses. Belfast City Council took over the Abbey Sanatorium in 1913 and renamed it the Belfast Municipal Sanatorium.

The pavilion system was part of the fresh-air treatment of the disease then fashionable.

 Elderly inmates of the Belfast Union Workhouse, c.1905, from a lantern slide. According to the report of the vice-regal commission on the Poor Law (1906), the Workhouse in March 1905 had 3,819 inmates, of whom 1,592 were sick, 1,476 aged or infirm, 174 lunatics or epileptics, 262 children and 315 able-bodied. The old women in their white bonnets can be seen in the background.

Laundry at the Edgar Home, Brunswick Street, Belfast, c.1901. Formerly the Ulster Female Penitentiary, this institution was established in 1839 'to receive penitent victims of seduction, and to encourage them to work for their own support within the walls of the institution, where there are extensive and appropriate facilities for washing, drying, mangling etc.'. It claimed to offer 'a refuge to all proper objects, without distinction of sect or party'. Fallen women did a lot of washing, it seems: the 'fallen and penitent females' of the Good Shepherd Convent also supported themselves by laundry work.

Men sleeping rough in the kilns of the Springfield Brickworks, c.1905. Hogg took this photograph at 3.30 a.m., for the Belfast Central Mission. He had other connections with the Mission, whose headquarters—the Grosvenor Hall in Grosvenor Road—was the venue for one of his regular weekly cinematograph shows; he also photographed the Mission's superintendent, the Rev. Dr Crawford Johnson.

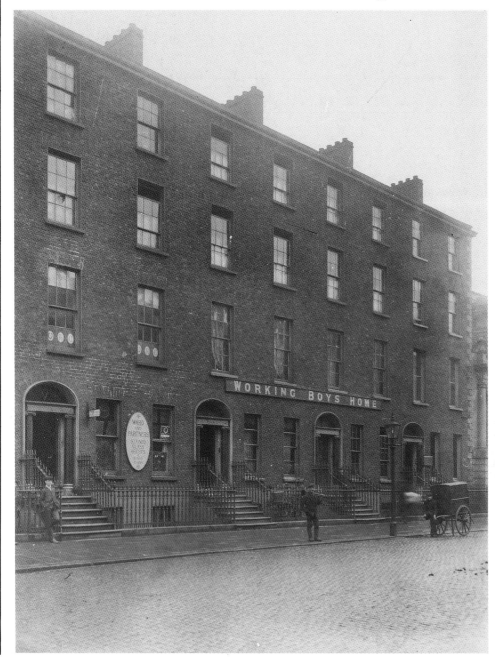

The Working Boys' Home, 27-29 May Street, 10 November 1909. According to the literature of the various societies that sought to help them, hundreds of homeless children roamed the streets of Belfast, many of them ending up in the courts.

The tea bar in Carrick House, Lower Regent Street, c.1907. Opened by the City Council in 1902 with accommodation for 100 men and later extended, this model lodging house was close to Hogg's studio in Trinity Street. Like a real bar in appearance—even to the foot rail—this one served only non-alcoholic drinks. The lodgers were encouraged to both inner cleanliness (Andrews' Liver Salts) and outer (Finlay's Soap).

HOUSE AND HOME

MANY OF HOGG'S PHOTOGRAPHS, like those of any photographer, show houses incidentally but were taken for some other reason. Many more, however, were specially commissioned either by public authorities or by private individuals. The most striking of those in the first category were taken in 1912 for the Corporation, as part of a survey of slum housing scheduled for demolition under the Belfast Improvement Order of 1910. Over-optimism among speculative builders in the 1890s led to more than 10,000 empty new houses in the city at the turn of the century, so the city fathers were in no hurry to build more at the expense of the ratepayers. Galvanised into action by a very critical government report of 1908, they agreed in 1910 to get rid of 700 or so of the worst houses in the old courts and alleys. Even then, the first of the new homes was not finished until 1917 because some councillors, concerned about their voting support, delayed the business. Other housing pictures were taken for architects, builders and property agents between the wars, when there was a considerable expansion of the residential suburbs on the north and south sides of the city.

Mitchell's Court, off Gardiner Street in the lower Shankill area, 9 March 1912, one of the streets scheduled for removal under the Improvement Order of 1910. The directories listed it only as 'four small houses'.

Beatty's Entry, off Hamill Street, 9 March 1912, from a lantern slide. The inhabitants of these 'few small houses' did not merit listing in the directory.

Johnstone's Court, off Millfield, 30 May 1912, from a lantern slide. Like Beatty's Entry, this was described only as 'a few small houses'. The gaunt mill building in the background adds much to the atmosphere.

Abbey Street, off Peter's Hill, 26 April 1912, from a lantern slide. 'A number of small houses' is how the directories described it. As in the case of the other three, the inhabitants were not listed.

Corporation housing at Seaview in July 1932. Though built by the Corporation, these houses were sold to private occupiers. Each cost £370, up to £350 of which was provided by an interest-free loan repayable over twenty-five years. Belfast had the worst record of any British city for municipal housebuilding between the wars. Only 2,562 were built, none after 1930, and that figure included the 374 at Seaview.

Lavinia Street, off the lower Ormeau Road, 15 June 1938, a photograph taken for the Concrete Piling Co. Ltd which was doing work in the area. Decent houses with their pedimented doors and good-sized windows, they were built in the 1870s, slightly later than those in Trinity Street where Hogg had his first studio. The second door in the picture led through to the back alley that was made compulsory under a local housing act of 1878, so that there would be direct access to privies.

New houses being built at Bawnmore Road, off the Lisburn Road, in 1920, from a lantern slide. This part of the city was developed between the wars by speculative builders, who produced homes such as these for the middle classes.

'Ideal Home': a display window at Campbell, Drennan & Co., house-furnishers, 36 Donegall Street in 1935. The settee and armchairs covered in Rexine, the Axminster carpet square, the light fittings, the dining furniture with metal trim, and the runner on the table are all as typical of certain rooms of the period as the picture rail, the door curtain to keep out draughts and the embossed paper on the ceiling.

Quintin Castle near Portaferry and its Old World Garden in 1925, from an album of prints taken for the King-Hall family. Magdalen King-Hall (Mrs Patrick Perceval-Maxwell), who appears in some of the pictures, started her career as a romantic novelist in 1925. Her later novel *Life and death of the wicked Lady Skelton* (1944) was made into a film starring Margaret Lockwood.

◻ The drawing room at Quintin Castle, 1925, from the same album. The
house is now a private nursing home.

EDUCATION

HOGG HAD HIS SHARE of conventional commissions from educational establishments of all kinds in Belfast—groups of staff and students, the opening ceremonies for new buildings and so on. Two particular clients, however, for whom he worked more systematically supply most of the photographs chosen for this section. One was the committee responsible for technical education in the city, to whom Hogg appears to have been official photographer throughout his career. The connection began at a time when the Municipal Technical Institute's activities were scattered in a number of unsatisfactory premises, which were soon to be replaced by a new College of Technology. Hogg probably lectured at the College to adult evening classes in photography. The other client was Dr W.A. McKeown, a well-known eye surgeon with strong and controversial views on the subject of primary education, with whom he carried out a survey of the city's National Schools in 1902. Nine of Hogg's photographs, in the form of photo engravings, were subsequently used to illustrate a lengthy interview with McKeown printed by the *Belfast Weekly Telegraph* (18 October 1902). As McKeown remarked, the photographs represented much better than he could do in words 'the terrible condition of child life in Belfast'. His criticism of clerical and sectarian control of schools did not endear him to the authorities: remarking that most of the Belfast schools were at the rear of churches and were uninviting in every respect, he went on: 'They occupy the same position in relation to churches as a gentleman's stable does to his private house'.

ROYAL ACADEMICAL INSTITUTION-BELFAST. A.R.Hogg Photo.

Front of the Royal Belfast Academical Institution, College Square, in 1902, shortly before the start of work on the new College of Technology, which has obscured the view of the right wing of this well-known boys' school for the past eighty years. Short of money, the school governors were tempted by a rent of £1,350 a year to lease the ground for ever in 1900. The old Municipal Technical Institute, now the north wing of the school, is just visible on the right.

The front of the Queen's University, Belfast in May 1914, with tennis matches in progress. The three Queen's Colleges at Belfast, Cork and Galway were established in 1845; the Belfast one had become a university in 1909. The Hamilton Tower (left) which marked the main entrance was built in 1907 and removed in 1922.

Cookery class in the old Municipal Technical Institute, College Square
North, c.1902.

Fig leaf department, College of Technology, c.1910.

Signwriting class in the College of Technology, 1910. That the 'nation' in the motto could be taken at that time to mean an undivided Ireland is indicated by the Irish welcome below, and by the celtic design on the right.

Examination in progress in the College of Technology's art department, 1910.

The training ship *Grampian* (formerly *Gibraltar*), moored in Belfast Lough, c.1899. Established in 1872 under the Industrial School (Ireland) Act of 1868 and supported by government grant and voluntary subscriptions, this ideal boarding school was for homeless and destitute boys. Every year, forty or fifty 'who have been rescued from a life of poverty and possible crime, and enabled to earn an honest living' were turned out to join the merchant marine; others were taught a trade. In 1899 the ship was sold for breaking up, after the boys had been transferred to Balmoral Industrial School.

Bootmaking class, Balmoral Industrial School, Belfast, c.1910, from a lantern slide. The Balmoral school—the only one in Ireland for protestant boys—was certified for 400 pupils. As another such establishment put it, the object was 'to rescue orphan, homeless and destitute street arab and criminal lads from the perils and temptations of street life; to educate them and teach them useful trades, so that, instead of becoming a terror to society, they may be brought up in health and happiness, to lead honest, useful lives in this world, and, with God's blessing, be fitted for another and a better'.

Teachers and pupils of Tullywest National School, near Ballynahinch, County Down, c.1902. The Hogg family came from Tullywest and Hogg himself was born there, though he never attended the little school. This conventional scene reveals no hint of rural tragedy: the principal (back row) was later dismissed and killed himself.

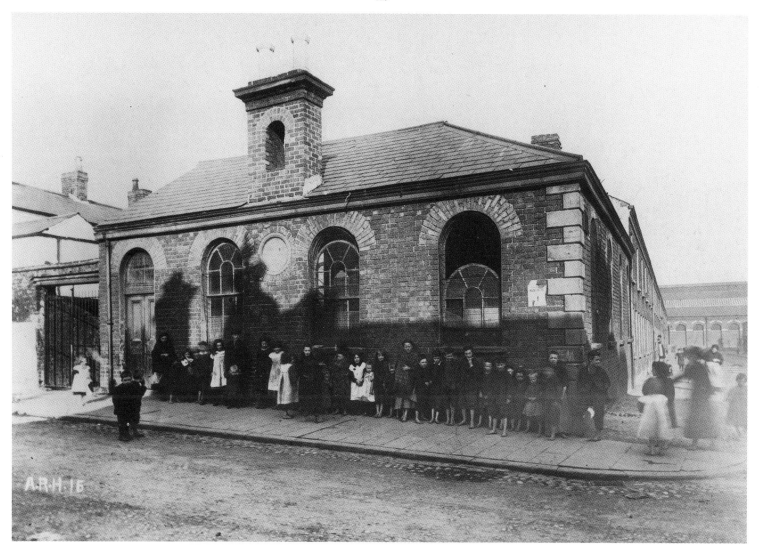

Conway Street (No.1) National School, off Falls Road, Belfast in 1902, from a lantern slide. This was one of the photographs taken by Hogg for Dr McKeown. The school was more than fifty years old at this date. McKeown's verdict on the city's schools was that 'most were so overcrowded, and contained such a pestilential atmosphere, that both the teachers and the children must have been so poisoned as to be unfit for any good intellectual work...'.

Springfield National School in 1902, from a lantern slide. This was one of the schools illustrated in the interview with Dr McKeown published by the *Belfast Weekly Telegraph*. It had one room, 178 pupils on its roll and space for no more than 125. Some of the children were 'half-timers', that is, they spent half the day at school and the other half working in a mill. As the caption of the newspaper illustration put it, 'The photograph shows the squalor and wretchedness, the broken walls, the patched windows, the children with bare feet and legs huddled together…'.

Forth River National School in 1902, from a lantern slide. The building may look derelict, but it was still in active operation when the photograph was taken. This was another newspaper illustration. The caption noted: 'There are 3 teachers in this hovel, 150 pupils on the roll, and space accommodation for 90'. Hogg's picture of the new building that eventually replaced it also survives.

Boys playing marbles in the playground of McQuiston National School, Oak Street in 1902, from a lantern slide. McQuiston was an example of one of the better schools in Dr McKeown's survey, for it had a playground whereas, he noted, 'the poor children of the National Schools as a rule have no playground but the street'. Compared with the children of Conway Street or Springfield, these boys are well-dressed and, because not forced out to work as soon as possible, significantly older. Was the lounging lad still a schoolboy? A monitor would have been expected to set a more upright example.

Boys in the playground of McQuiston National School in 1902. The game
they are simulating for the photographer is a robust kind of leap-frog sometimes
known as 'Churchie'.

RELIGION

DURING HOGG'S LIFETIME organised religion occupied a very important part in Irish society and in the lives of a great many people. This fact is reflected in his photographs. Since Belfast was predominantly a protestant—indeed presbyterian—city, and he himself an orthodox presbyterian, most of Hogg's photographs of religious institutions, activities and people inevitably portray aspects of protestantism. Protestantism was so fragmented, however, that the variety of the photographs dealing with it is still considerable. Hogg's personal acquaintance among protestant church people ranged from the clergy of Belfast's major churches and missions to the pastors and officials of some of its astonishing variety of evangelical sects. Such was his reputation as a photographer that his commissions were by no means entirely confined to these sources, as is shown by the pictures of the Leitrim grotto.

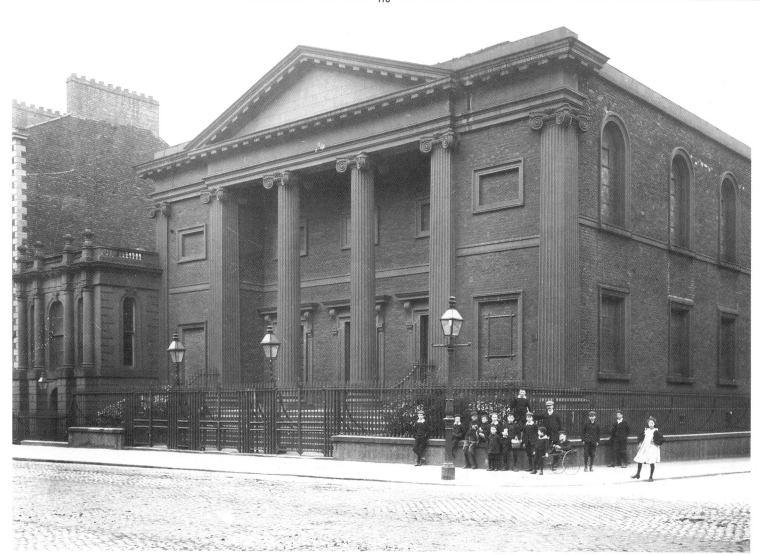

A view of the parish church at Knockbreda, County Down, August 1916. The church was designed by Richard Castle, an eighteenth-century architect better known for great houses such as Leinster House in Dublin. This fine picture by Hogg was later used as the frontispiece to the history of the parish.

May Street Presbyterian Church, 1902. Built in 1829 in the classical style then favoured by presbyterians, May Street's first minister (till his death in 1868) was the redoubtable Dr Henry Cooke. By 1902 May Street itself and the streets around it were no longer inhabited by the well-to-do middle classes (the ministers of the church themselves had been living in the leafy suburbs for some time). The local children appear to be very respectable nevertheless.

Evangelist at work outside the Campbell Street Mission, off Old Lodge Road, 2 April 1932.

Interior of the Elim Pentecostal Tabernacle, Hunter Street, 10 April 1935. The lack of aesthetic trappings common to all gospel halls is carried to the extreme here, where nothing distracts the hearers from the Word.

☐ Eloquent silence: a sermon at the Institution for the Deaf and Dumb, Lisburn Road, Belfast in August 1939. This must have been one of Hogg's last pictures.

☐ Hungry sheep: a gospel mission in the Central Market, Portadown, County Armagh, in March 1931.

Blessing the new grotto at St Mary's Church, Leitrim, County Down, 26
May 1929, from an album of prints.

Another picture of the Lourdes grotto at Leitrim, taken on the same occasion.

Group of clergy who attended the blessing of the grotto at Leitrim, 26 May 1929.

Four Presbyterian clergy at Boardmills, County Down, 30 July 1924. The first three from the right were Revs Moody (Boardmills), Dickson (Saintfield) and Kelso (Boardmills).

ENTERTAINMENT

DURING THE FIRST forty years of this century, public entertainment was transformed by the arrival of the cinema. Hogg himself was keenly interested in cinematography, and in the early part of his career as a photographer he provided regular weekly shows, as well as offering his services to anyone in town or country who was prepared to hire him. Later, when the spread of the commercial cinema had put an end to such occasional work, he received commissions to photograph many of the places that had put him out of business; several of the resulting pictures, so reminiscent of the period between the wars, survive in the collection. So too do photographs of the traditional theatres that preceded them. Then, from its establishment in 1924, the Belfast station of the British Broadcasting Company (renamed Corporation when it became a public concern in 1926) provided him with a considerable amount of new work of a different kind.

The Royal Hippodrome and the Palace of Varieties, Great Victoria Street, c.1907. The Grand Opera House, opened in 1895, was known as the Palace of Varieties for the five years 1904-09. Its neighbour and rival the Hippodrome was built in 1905. The overhead wires for the electric trams also indicate a date of 1906 at the earliest. By ignoring the photographer's need for his subjects to stand still or to move slowly, the cow has acquired an extra leg.

The audience at the Grand Opera House, Saturday 4 August 1917. The performance was the last night of 'A Royal Divorce', a popular tale of Napoleon and Josephine. Incidental music was provided by the band of the Royal Irish Constabulary, which played 'The Battle of Waterloo'. Several of the couples in the front stalls on the left are carefully hiding their faces from the camera. Hogg took this photograph with a camera which held a glass plate negative measuring 15 inches by 12.

◻ Jimmy O'Dea in 'Ali Baba' at the Empire Theatre, 6 December 1936. The first performance to be broadcast from any Irish theatre, the revue 'Hip, hip, hooradio', was relayed by the BBC from the stage of the Empire in December 1927.

◻ The Alhambra Theatre, North Street, as a cinema, December 1937. Founded in 1873, the Alhambra was a successful—and sometimes scandalous—music hall before competition from the Empire obliged it to seek a new audience. Films were shown here from 1907.

Kelvin Picture Palace, College Square East, undated but c.1911. This is the earliest known photograph of a Belfast cinema. It was named after William Thomson, Lord Kelvin, the distinguished scientist, who was born in one of these houses in 1824 and spent his early years there. The cinema put on three shows a day, and seats cost 6d. and 3d.

Exterior of the Picturedrome Cinema, Mountpottinger Road, 12 April 1935. This is one of a number of similar pictures taken by Hogg of the new-style luxury cinemas that appeared in Belfast in the 1930s.

Foyer of the Stadium Cinema, Shankill Road, November 1937.

British Broadcasting Company concert party, outside the studio in Linenhall Street, Belfast in 1925. The young man in shirtsleeves and bow tie on the right is Tyrone Guthrie, the great theatrical producer whose first job after leaving Oxford in 1924 was as junior assistant to the director of the new broadcasting station in Belfast. The play that is being rehearsed was entitled 'A Trip to the Isle of Man'. The photograph was presumably taken for publicity.

Shankill Road Mission gym group dancing to glory, 1931.

B.B.C. cabaret girls at the Grand Central Hotel, Royal Avenue in 1937.

SHOPS AND ADVERTISING

MANY ASPECTS of the commercial life of Belfast are illustrated in the Hogg collection. This section includes a few of the photographs featuring shops and advertising. Such commissions are an important part of any commercial photographer's work. Like other premises, shops were often photographed just before being knocked down or altered. New shops were frequently recorded, especially if their architecture or construction were notably modern. To give an example not represented in this selection, several of the new chain stores that appeared in British high streets between the wars—Woolworth's, Saxone, Austin Reed—were photographed by Hogg for owners, architects or builders. The pictures presented here, however, are less concerned with the architecture of shops than with their activities.

The advertising and promotion of goods brought an increasing amount of work to photographers as the technical problems of reproducing photographs for trade purposes were solved. As advertising itself became more highly organised, firms such as Allen's and Eason's employed Hogg to record their displays. Promoters of the use of electricity, and of the new wireless, were particularly quick to see the benefits of publicity illustrated by photographs.

◻ A corner of the covered market at Smithfield, c.1910.

The post office in Sandy Row, Belfast, 28 December 1937.

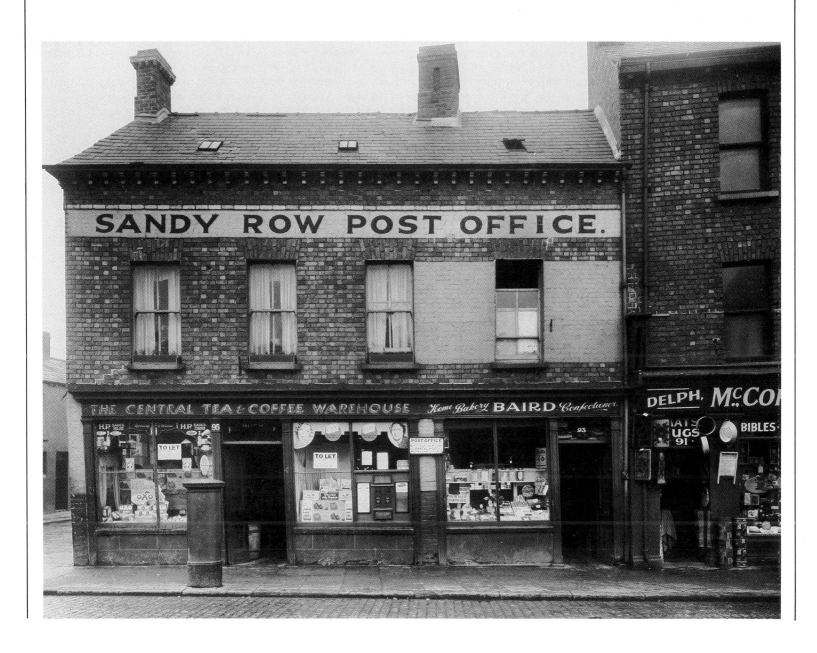

□ Ulster Industries Development Association advertisement somewhere in Belfast, 1934. Taken along with the previous one, this photograph neatly illustrates one of the effects of the partition of Ireland. It is also a fine example of 1930s design.

□ 'Irish Exhibition' at the offices of the Belfast Industrial Development Association, Queen Street, c.1905.

Johnston's umbrella shop, 31 High Street, Belfast, 1935. Johnston's are still in business but are now in Ann Street. Next door at No. 29 was the photographic studio of William Abernethy, which was established there in 1886.

W.R. Rangecroft's shop at 229 Antrim Road, April 1931.

Castle Arcade, Castle Place, Belfast in 1930. The clock in the ceiling was (though not literally) a striking feature of the arcade's modern design.

Radio exhibition in the Plaza Ballroom, Chichester Street, Belfast,
September 1936.

 Window display at W. Erskine Mayne's bookshop in Donegall Square West in 1935.

Window of Belfast Corporation Electricity showrooms at 9 Wellington Place, 1 September 1936.

Listening to the wireless, August 1931, an
advertisement for headphones as an aid to
family harmony.

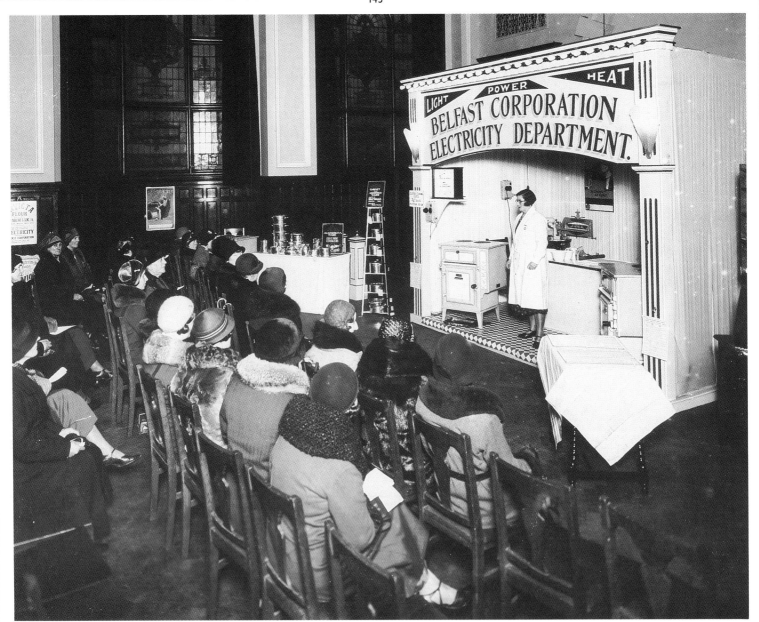

Belfast Corporation Electricity Department demonstration at the College of Technology, 28 November 1932.

Interior of the General Electric Company's showrooms, 9-15 Queen Street,
17 February 1932.

OTELS AND EATING PLACES

LIKE SHOPKEEPERS, owners of hotels and restaurants of all kinds frequently employed photographers to record the appearance, attractions and activities of their premises, because they were anxious to bring them to the notice of the public whose custom they sought. Hogg received a large number of commissions of this sort during the forty years of his career. In addition, he sometimes photographed such places incidentally when engaged on other work. Many of the resulting negatives have survived in the Hogg collection. These pictures can be an exceptionally evocative source for the social historian.

International Temperance Hotel, College Square East, 1902. Hogg took a number of large-format photographs of the site of the new College of Technology and the buildings around it in College Square. Staying at the International in 1906 cost six shillings a day ('minimum terms for two in each bed'). There were large numbers of temperance hotels and restaurants in Belfast at the time: the delegates to the British Convention of the Christian Endeavour movement which met in the city in 1899 had a wide choice of suitable lodgings and eating houses.

The Grand Central Hotel, Royal Avenue, September 1929. Built in 1893, during the development of Royal Avenue, for a central railway station that was never built, the hotel with its 200 bedrooms was for many years the most luxurious in Belfast. It was demolished in 1985, after ten years as Army quarters.

Lounge of the Grand Central Hotel with musical quintet and a selection of lounge lizards, 24 October 1932.

Afternoon tea on the verandah of Rosapenna Hotel, County Donegal c.1919. This hotel was much frequented by visitors from eastern Ulster, and much photographed by R.J. Welch as well as Hogg.

Bedroom in the Presbyterian War Memorial Hostel, Howard Street, 3 March 1932. Opened in that year, the Hostel provided spartan quarters for generations of students and others in need of cheap, respectable (and unlicensed) lodgings in the city.

Milk Bar in Lombard Street, 19 May 1938. The milk bar was attached to the Lombard Cafe, a temperance establishment. Hogg took photographs of this and similar places for the Ministry of Agriculture.

Milk Bar in Great Victoria Street, 27 September 1937.

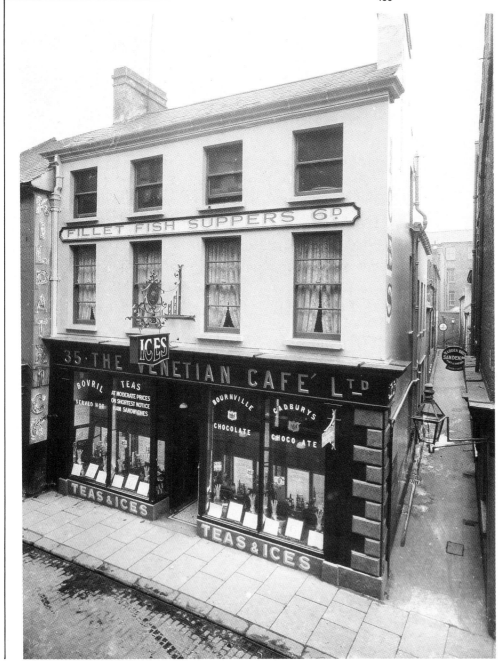

The Venetian Cafe, 35-37 Church Lane in 1935. The Venetian was one of a number of cafes opened by Italian immigrants in Belfast and other towns in the north of Ireland. In the 1920s, before it got a bad name in democratic circles everywhere, fascism flourished among the Italian community. A party of Italian Fascists paraded and laid a wreath at the unveiling of the war memorial in Belfast in 1929 (so too did units of the Ulster Women's branch of the British Fascist Party).

City Oyster Rooms, 7-11 William Street South c.1902. This section of the restaurant trade was evidently at a low ebb, the area about to be redeveloped. In their heyday, Mrs Mitchell's Fish and Oyster establishments in Castle Lane, Castle Market and William Street advertised a constant supply of all kinds of fish in season and 'gentlemen favouring her with their orders' might rely upon 'her most particular attention'.

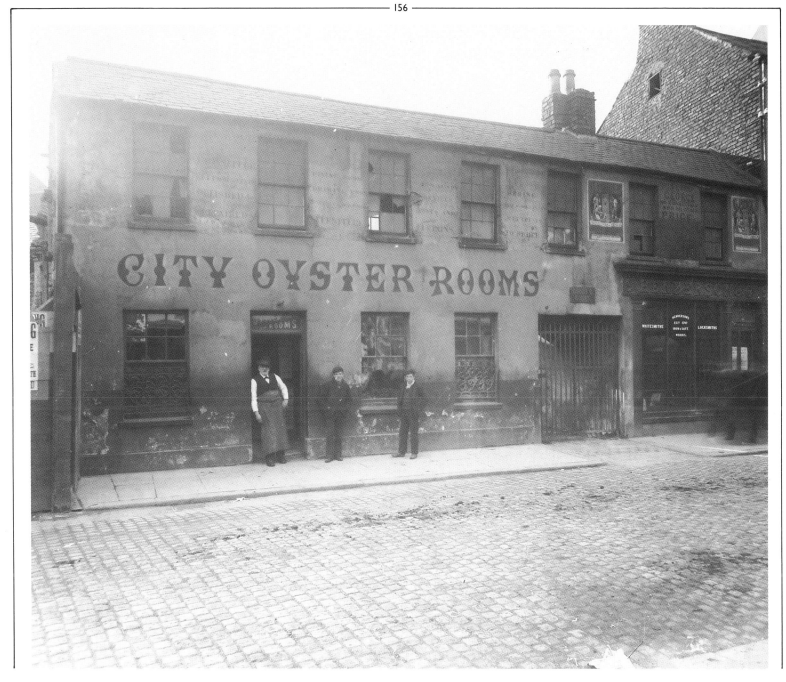

The Dub Tea Rooms on the Upper Malone Road c.1910. The Tea Rooms were within easy walking distance of the tram terminus at Malone Park and catered for city dwellers on afternoon rambles.

Exterior of the Carlton Cafe and Restaurant, Donegall Place, in 1931. The Carlton was a favourite meeting place for the respectable citizens of Belfast between the wars, and Hogg took many pictures there.

■ Interior of the Carlton, 9 December 1936, with the Hoover Company's dinner and ball in progress.

■ The Cafe Royal, a temperance cafe on the ground floor of the Y.M.C.A. Building, Wellington Place, April 1933.

CITY SCENES

NOTHING DISAPPEARS MORE QUICKLY—and nothing is more difficult to reconstruct from non-visual evidence—than the actual appearance of places in the past. The unique contribution of photography to the study of history lies in providing the historian with the visual appearance of things (and people) at a particular point in time. Hogg's photographs give the local historian many glimpses of the physical appearance of Belfast between the turn of the century and the outbreak of the Second World War. Nor is the interest of such glimpses entirely confined to the local historian: as one of the great industrial city ports of the British Isles, Belfast had important features in common with Glasgow, Liverpool and other places.

◻ View from the College of Technology, 27 June 1930. The outstanding landmarks visible are the twin spires of St Peter's pro-cathedral in Derby Street and Hughes' great flour mill. The houses in the foreground were in College Square North.

☐ Queen's Bridge from the County Antrim side, May 1909. The jetty for the Bangor boat is on the left, Kelly's coal yards across the river. As well as the open-topped electric tram, there is a variety of horse-drawn (and small-boy-drawn) vehicles on the roadway, but not a motor vehicle in sight.

Floods in Donegall Square, September 1902, from a lantern slide. A new system of sewers was unable to cope with heavy rain and an usually high tide, with the result that a mixture of rainwater, seawater and sewage swilled around in the city centre. Note the horse tram and the hoardings round the site of the City Hall.

⬚ The view of Donegall Square and Donegall Place from the front of the new City Hall in 1906. Robinson & Cleaver's great department store (right) went out of business in 1984. In those days, as the awning on the right proclaims, they were manufacturers to the King—manufacturers of linen, some of which was made on the premises by hand-loom weavers who worked on the top floor. The father and children in the foreground have evidently come to see Queen Victoria and the City Hall.

A.R.HOGG. 28.MAY.1903.

■ The new City Hall under construction, 28 May 1903. Built on the site of the eighteenth century White Linen Hall, this splendid building was finished in 1906. Beyond it on the left can be seen some of the few remaining Georgian houses which once made up Donegall Square.

The City Hall as it looked when just completed, in 1906. The gardeners had just finished doing the flower beds, their wheelbarrows and implements still scattered about. The exceptional quality of the picture is due to the large size of the negative. Hogg took this and many other fine pictures of the building for the official brochure that was published to mark the opening.

 Falls Road public baths and free library, undated but c.1910, from a lantern slide.

 The river Lagan below Ormeau Bridge at low tide, c.1908, with the city gasworks in the background, from a lantern slide. Passengers from Ormeau Park are seen queueing for the rowboat ferry that plied across the river at this point for many years.

Remnant and old clothes market in Belfast in 1899, from a lantern slide.
Secondhand clothing played an important part in the domestic life of the poorer
classes of society, and in the lower reaches of the city's economy.

Fire at Marsh's Biscuit Factory, Clifton Street, 1905. The horse-drawn fire
brigade (it became motorised five years later) is in action, watched by a large
crowd. The small boys in this and similar pictures of the period may frequently
be barefooted, but they are never without caps. The fire at Marsh's provided
Hogg with a convenient news photograph: his studio in Trinity Street was just
round the corner.

❑ Donegall Square West from Donegall Square South in the early 1920s. The fine building on the corner of Howard Street (left) was built as a linen warehouse; next door was a branch of the Northern Bank. Between that and the imposing bulk of the Scottish Provident Building were the last of the Georgian houses on this side of the square.

❑ Kiln of Ballymacarrett glassworks, 7 January 1930. Described in the local press at the time of its erection by John Smylie in 1785 as the largest in the British Isles, with a height of 150 feet and a circumference of 180, this was the first of three kilns built in the late eighteenth century and the early 1800s. One had gone by 1823 and a second was removed in the mid-nineteenth century. This one, stranded in the yard of Richardson's Chemical Manure Co., collapsed on 11 October 1937. Flint glassmaking at Belfast went through very chequered times before coming to an end in 1868.

❏ View of Bradbury Place. The picture is not dated but from clues such as the new-style tram with covered top deck (introduced in 1910), the motor car and the dresses of the women it must have been taken about 1911. The curious little house on the left, removed some years ago to make way for a redevelopment which has not yet taken place, was the toll house for the Belfast-Lisburn turnpike.

Snowscape in Belfast, 12 March 1937, taken from the back of Hogg's studio and home at 67 Great Victoria Street.

OCCASIONS

EVER SINCE ITS EARLY DAYS, photography has been used increasingly to record public occasions of all kinds. In fact, the earliest original negative in the Ulster Museum's collections is one taken in College Square in 1855 at the unveiling of the statue of Frederick Richard, Earl of Belfast (the original 'Black Man', before his statue was replaced by that of Dr Cooke). This short section contains a few of the pictures taken by Hogg on various occasions during his career.

'Miss Belfast 1927' in a linen industry parade, outside the College of Technology.

Official opening of the Dufferin hospital for children at the Belfast Workhouse infirmary in 1909. The Board of Guardians had decided in 1905 to replace the crowded and insanitary wards of the children's infirmary. The new hospital had 78 beds and an operating theatre on its three floors. Lady Hermione Blackwood, daughter of the first Marquess of Dufferin and Ava, performed the opening ceremony.

King Edward VII and Queen Alexandra at the unveiling of the statue of
Queen Victoria, in front of the partially -built City Hall in Belfast, 27 July 1903.

The unveiling of the memorial to Frederick Hamilton Temple Blackwood, first Marquess of Dufferin and Ava, by the Marquess of Londonderry, at the new City Hall, 9 June 1906. This splendid crowd scene is one of Hogg's large-plate photographs.

Volunteers of the 3rd battalion, North Belfast Ulster Volunteer Force, parading in the grounds of Belfast Castle in 1913.

Platform party at an Ulster Unionist meeting in the Ulster Hall, Belfast, 27 September 1912. This meeting was the climax of the campaign leading up to the Solemn League and Covenant, which was signed next day by the Unionist leaders at the City Hall. The slogan above the platform was coined by the Duke of Abercorn twenty years earlier, at the time of the second Home Rule Bill.

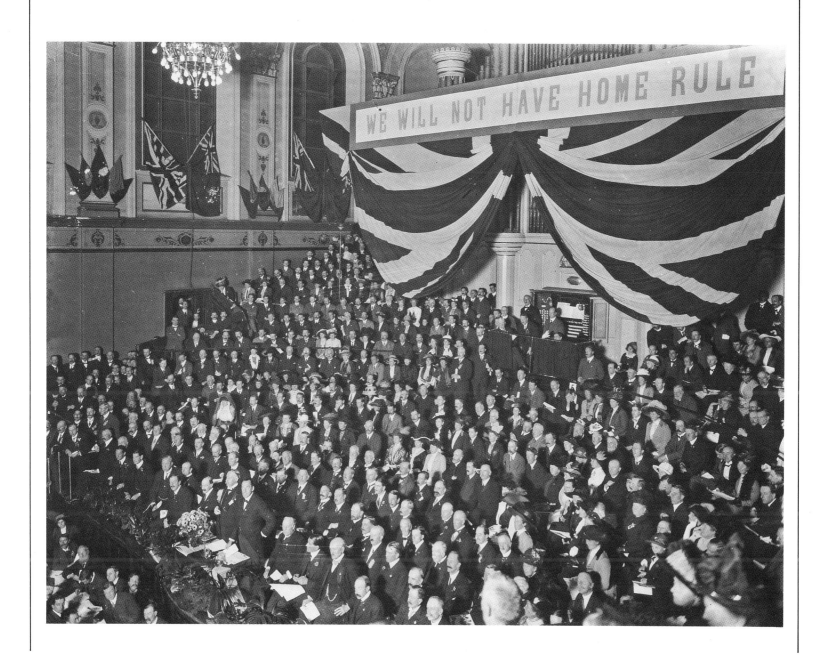

 Unveiling of the statue of Lord Kelvin in the Botanic Gardens, Belfast in June 1913. William Thomson, Baron Kelvin of Largs, was born in College Square East in 1824 and died at his home in Scotland in 1907. Appointed professor of natural philosophy at Glasgow University at the age of twenty-two, he held the chair until 1899 and subsequently became chancellor of the university. Among other distinctions, he was one of the original members of the Order of Merit (1902).

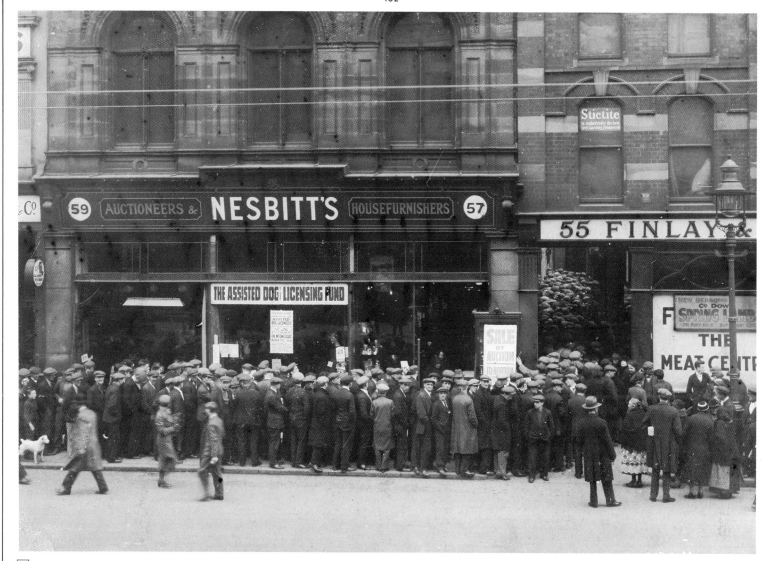

■ Unemployed men—and one dog—queueing in High Street, Belfast, 15 March 1933. The notice in the window reads: 'Applicants for assisted dog licenses must apply in person and pay 2/6 at 57 High Street on Wednesday March 15th at 3 p.m. No claims will be considered after the date. Applicants who are in employment need not apply'. The large number of applicants is a curious illustration of the numbers of unemployed in Belfast in the 1930s—and of their willingness to conform to the licensing regulations.

FACES

ALTHOUGH HOGG did not set out to be a portrait photographer, he was always willing to take pictures of individuals and groups. In the early part of his career, when his studio was in Trinity Street, he did comparatively little work of this kind. The move to a city centre studio in 1921 brought much more of it his way. Many of his sitters in the 1920s were fellow members of the Belfast Art Society, the Ulster Arts Club, the Rotary Club or other organisations. The quality of his work explains why, although not a portrait specialist, he obtained so many portrait commissions. These last examples of his work fittingly complete a book which reflects his very varied achievement.

Bernard Gorman, said to be one hundred years old, at the door of his cottage at Proud-footstown in the Boyne valley. Hogg took his photograph in 1899 or 1900.

Robert Ponsonby Staples at work on his triptych of Belfast harbour, c.1905.
The three panels (from left) show workers making turbines at Workman Clark's
yard; the liner *Amerika* on the stocks at Harland & Wolff's; and passengers,
including three of the artist's daughters, boarding the Bangor boat. Originally
intended for the new City Hall, the painting is now in the Ulster Museum.
Among his many forgotten works is *England v. Australia 1887*, which hangs in
the Memorial Gallery at Lord's cricket ground. Staples, who came of a land-
owning family in County Tyrone, succeeded to a baronetcy at the age of eighty.
His eccentricities included walking barefoot on the tramlines in the belief that
electricity would thus enter his system and do him good.

Lady Whitla in her house at Lennoxvale, Belfast, c.1907. Sir William Whitla was for many years professor of pharmacology at Queen's College and at Queen's University. After retiring from his chair he was elected M.P. for the university seat at Westminster. He died in 1933, leaving to Queen's University substantial endowments and his house (now the residence of the vice-chancellor). Lady Whitla was a formidable figure in her own right. A member of the Salvation Army, she once attended a royal garden party wearing its uniform.

R.J. Hall, amateur artist and member of the Belfast Art Society, in the
drawing room of his house at Crumlin Road, Belfast c.1905.

Rosamond Praeger, the sculptress, in her studio at Holywood, County
Down, undated but probably sometime during the 1920s. The figures of children
are very characteristic of her work, which was widely admired.

 Judge Brown, 1936. Thomas Watters Brown (1879-1944), fifth and youngest son of a Newtownards draper, was called to the Irish bar in 1907, took silk in 1918, in which year he was also elected Unionist M.P. for North Down, and was appointed Solicitor General (the last for the whole of Ireland) in 1921. He was a high court judge for Northern Ireland from 1922 till his death.

The artist Paul Henry posing with a portrait of his brother, Professor R.M. Henry, 21 July 1933.

Father E. McGivern, parish priest of
Ballynahinch, County Down, 22nd May 1932.

An outing of the Belfast Art Society at Sketrick Castle, County Down c.1910. The figure fifth from the left, kneeling penitentially on a stone, looks like Hogg himself. Apart from a montage portrait of one of his artist friends, done in 1925, there is no evidence that Hogg produced any paintings, but he was a keen member of the Society from 1902.

Millers and grain merchants golf competition, Newcastle, 30 May 1906.

Belfast Naturalists' Field Club outing at Crebilly House, County Antrim, 29 June 1907. The last figure on the right in the front row, with his hat on his foot, is Hogg's fellow member and fellow photographer R.J. Welch.

Group of men at Belfast Dog Show in 1909.

The Rev. Dr R. Crawford Johnson, Methodist minister and superintendent of the Grosvenor Hall Mission, at home with his womenfolk in Wellington Park, c.1909.

Staff of W. Dobbin & Co., grocers and chemists, North Street, Belfast, c.1907. Hogg worked in Dobbin's as a druggist before setting up as a photographer, and for many years photographed outings and other events for the Chemists and Druggists Society.

Sportsmen of Harland & Wolff's shipyard, c.1915.

No hothouse blooms, though all under cloches: lady members of Balmoral
Golf Club, 14 September 1929.

The Vallely family, about to emigrate from Belfast, 4 May 1929. In April
and May of that year Hogg took a number of similar groups on the quayside for
McCalla & Co., shipping agents.

The McVeeters family, emigrants, 11 May 1929.

❏ The Bennett family, emigrants, 20 April 1929.

❏ Group of women workers at Loopbridge Weaving factory, Lismore Street, Belfast, 12 May 1937. The decorations were for the coronation of George VI.

'The Rising Moon', a view of Belfast Lough and harbour, c.1895.